People of the Ancient World

THE ANCIENT MAYA

WRITTEN BY
LILA PERL

Franklin Watts
A Division of Scholastic Inc.
New York Toronto London Auckland Sydney
Mexico City New Delhi Hong Kong
Danbury, Connecticut

Note to readers: Definitions for words in bold can be found in the Glossary at the back of this book.

Photographs © 2005: AKG-Images, London: 48, 95 top, 100 top (Andrea Baguzzi), 30 (Françios Guénet); Art Resource, NY: 33, 86, 100 bottom (Werner Forman), 65 (Erich Lessing); Aurora/Peter McBride: 46, 95 bottom left; Bridgeman Art Library International Ltd., London/New York: 88 (Bibliotheque Nationale, Paris, France/Archives Charmet), 96 (Ian Mursell/Mexicolore), 76 (Musee de l'Homme, Paris, France/Giraudon), 23, 94 bottom (Museum of Fine Arts, Houston, Texas, USA), 89 (Museum of Fine Arts, Houston, Texas, USA/Funds provided by the Alice Pratt Brown Museum Fund), 9 (Private Collection); Corbis Images: 17 (Archivo Iconografico, S.A.), 58 (Richard A. Cooke), 51 (Sergio Dorantes), 4 center, 92 top left (Macduff Everton), 15 top right, 16, 24, 44 (Charles & Josette Lenars); Getty Images/Orlando Sierra/AFP: 93; Justin Kerr: 21, 28; Landov, LLC: 57, 61, 95 bottom right, 101 (Rauchwetter/dpa); Lonely Planet Images: 78 (Kim Grant), 99 (Alfredo Maiquez); National Geographic Image Collection: 37 (Enrico Ferorelli), 63, 96 bottom (Raymond Gehman), 80 (Terry W. Rutledge), 82 (Doug Stern); Peter Arnold Inc.: 19 (Martha Cooper), 41 (Douglas Waugh); Philip Baird/www.anthroarcheart.org: 34; The Art Archive/Picture Desk: 26, 43 (Archaeological and Ethnological Museum Guatemala City/Dagli Orti), 72, 94 top (Archaeological Museum Copan Honduras), 7 (Biblioteca Nacional Mexico/Dagli Orti), 53 (National Anthropological Museum Mexico/Dagli Orti), 91 (Yucatan Research Centre Mexico/Mireille Vautier); The British Museum: 35, 100 center (Gift of A.P. Maudslay); The Image Works: 10 (ARPL/Topham), 31 (Macduff Everton), 67 (Tony Savino), 98 (The British Museum).

Cover art by Paine Proffitt
Map by XNR Productions Inc.

Library of Congress Cataloging-in-Publication Data

Perl, Lila.
   The ancient Maya / Lila Perl.
           p. cm. — (People of the ancient world)

Includes bibliographical references and index.
ISBN 0-531-12381-2 (lib. bdg.)   0-531-16848-4 (pbk.)
1. Mayas—History—Juvenile literature. 2. Mayas—Social life and customs—Juvenile literature. I. Title. II. Series.
F1435.P47 2005
972.81'016—dc22

                                                                        2004026379

Contents

HOW WE KNOW ABOUT THE ANCIENT MAYA

A lost city in the jungle. This was the image that lured the American explorer John Lloyd Stephens to the ruins of an ancient Maya city and ceremonial site in the Central American nation of Honduras in the year 1839. Photography was in its infancy in 1839, so traveling with Stephens was the renowned English artist Frederick Catherwood.

The two men sailed from New York City, arrived at the Caribbean port of Belize City (in present-day Belize), and made their way inland on foot and with pack mules, traveling through tangled undergrowth and across muddy rivers. They were plagued by intense heat and humidity, poisonous snakes, and biting insects.

When they at last reached the fabled city, which they had learned about from both Maya and Spanish sources of the day, they found it to be overgrown with giant trees, vines, roots, and saplings. It was badly eroded by one thousand years of continued exposure to the

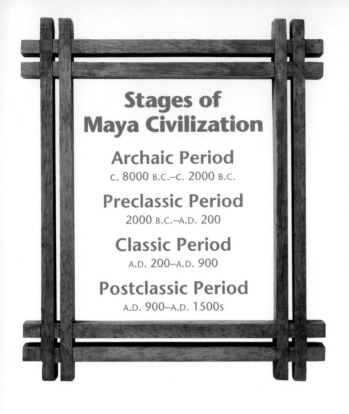

Stages of Maya Civilization

Archaic Period
c. 8000 B.C.–c. 2000 B.C.

Preclassic Period
2000 B.C.–A.D. 200

Classic Period
A.D. 200–A.D. 900

Postclassic Period
A.D. 900–A.D. 1500s

elements. It was, in fact, difficult to recognize as the onetime site of great plazas flanked with soaring stone structures—temple platforms and stepped pyramids—carved with undecipherable symbols believed to be a form of writing.

The only sign of life near the site of the ancient city was a village of people of mixed native Mesoamerican and Spanish stock. (Mesoamerica is generally identified as southeastern Mexico and Central America.) In order to be able to employ people to clear some of the jungle growth and to work undisturbed at excavating the carved stone pillars, known as **stelae**, Stephens bought the ruined site from the local chieftain. The site took its name from the nearby village of Copán.

As Stephens later wrote in his two-volume *Incidents of Travel in Central America, Chiapas, and Yucatan*, published in 1841, "I paid fifty dollars for Copán. There was never any difficulty about the price. I offered that sum, for which Don José María thought me only a fool; if I had offered more he would probably have considered me something worse."

From the fall of 1839 to the spring of 1840, Stephens and Catherwood tried to unveil the architecture, take measurements, and make drawings of the ruins of Copán. But the task of rescuing the great monuments, the plazas, and even the smaller commemorative stelae from the tropical forest was overwhelming. The two men could only guess at what Copán might have looked like in ancient times. When had that been? How long had the great ceremonial city held sway? What had happened to its populace, its officials, its priests, and its rulers? And what had caused it to fall into desolation and ruin?

Nor could Stephens and Catherwood explain how the ancient Maya, who did not have beasts of burden, had transported stones from quarries, carved them without metal tools, or erected tall structures with them. Least of all, what did the ornate and finely detailed carvings of figures, decorative elements, and squares full of symbols that appeared to be a form of writing mean?

Beyond Copán

Copán was not the only ancient Maya site that Stephens and Catherwood were to explore. As time went on, it was learned that there were some sixty such sites, or city-states. Meanwhile, in April 1840, the two journeyed by land over mountainous terrain and through rain forest to the Mexican state of Chiapas, where the

An engraving by Frederick Catherwood shows the arch of Labna built by the Maya.

fabled Maya center of Palenque lay in yet another tangle of deep jungle. Their stay at Palenque, however, was short, for the explorers were suffering from symptoms of malaria and exhaustion. In June, they sailed from the coast of the Gulf of Mexico to the less tropical plain of Mexico's Yucatán Peninsula, and from there home to New York City, arriving in July 1840.

The nineteenth-century explorers had taken only a preliminary look at a civilization that arose in Mesoamerica as early as 2000 B.C., that reached its apex, or Classic Period, between A.D. 200 and A.D. 900, and that survived in only slightly altered form until the Spanish conquest in the 1500s.

Maya culture had many characteristics. Like some of their Mexican neighbors, the Maya built great stone pyramids and ceremonial centers, they practiced human sacrifice and personal bloodletting, and they revered a pantheon of gods. They also played a ritual ball game that had serious consequences for the losers, and they were active as traders and merchants and above all as warriors and priests.

The Maya also had attributes and accomplishments that were unique. They studied the skies to help them understand the movements of the stars and the planets and were able to track the stations of Venus and Mars with amazing accuracy. They understood not only the phases of the moon and the solar year, but could predict lunar and solar eclipses. They built observatories onto some of their stone structures, and they constructed various temples so that they would be in alignment with dramatic features of the heavens at certain times of the year.

In addition to their achievements in astronomy, the Maya had a complex calendar that included both sacred and civil aspects, and they developed a system of counting and recording time that included the concept of zero. The zero was formerly believed to

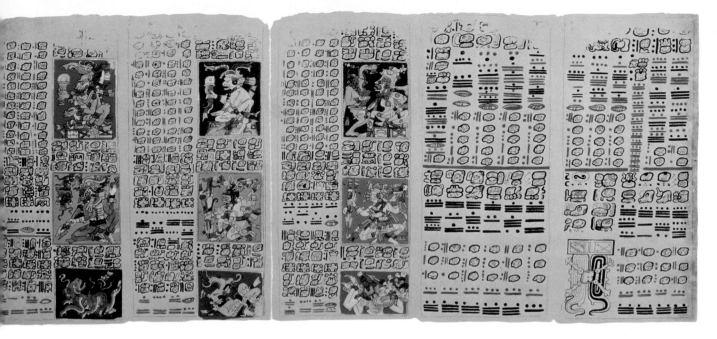

A copy of a Maya manuscript shows astronomical calculations.

have been the invention solely of the Hindus in the 100s B.C. and was unknown in Europe until the late Middle Ages (but long known by then by the Maya).

Outstanding among their neighbors, the Maya had a highly developed writing system that used **hieroglyphs**, which were not only inscribed or painted on stone monuments, ceramic pottery, and objects of wood, bone, shell, and jade, but were recorded on fig-bark paper or deerskin and folded accordion-style to form books called codices (the plural of **codex**).

The explorations of Stephens and Catherwood continued with one more trip to the Yucatán, where there were a number of Maya ceremonial sites in somewhat better condition than the badly overgrown and abandoned Copán and Palenque. In 1843, Stephens published his *Incidents of Travel in the Yucatan.* Stephens, who died of malaria in 1852 at the age of forty-seven, was never to return to the Maya lands. But his efforts to learn about the largely vanished past of an important civilization earned him the title of "the father of Maya archaeology."

Surviving Maya Writings

The four codices that are known today have survived in manuscript form and date from the Postclassic Period. They are known as the Dresden, Paris, Madrid, and Grolier codices. The Dresden Codex, which turned up in Vienna in 1739, deals mainly with prophecies as related to Maya astronomy. Similarly, the fragmentary Paris Codex, discovered in 1859, and the Madrid Codex, found in two parts in the 1860s, both predict the future based on the 260-day divinatory, or sacred, calendar of the Maya. The Grolier Codex was found in Mexico in 1965 and deals largely with the study of the planet Venus. The Madrid Codex, with fifty-six leaves painted on both sides, is the longest.

We also know about the Maya from early post-conquest works that were written in the Yucatán in the 1600s and were translated from the Mayan language. Known as *The Books of Chilam B'alam*, they are mainly prophecies by the local shamans, or seers, of the Yucatán communities. The *Popol Vuh*, on the other hand, was written by the Quiché Maya of the Guatemala highlands and is a poem of more than nine thousand lines describing the origin of the universe as viewed by the ancient Maya, as well as their mythology and history. This literary work is based on both oral tradition and on pre-conquest written sources.

Historians, archaeologists, geologists, climatologists, engineers, photographers, plant and soil specialists, and epigraphers (hieroglyphic scholars who study inscriptions) were among those who now joined the ranks of those who sought to understand the origins and the development of the great Classic Period of the Maya.

Learning About the Maya from the Spanish

The contact that had taken place between the Maya of the Late Postclassic Period and the officials and clergy of the Spanish conquest during the 1500s was an important key to unlocking the Maya's past. A leading figure on Mexico's Maya-populated Yucatán Peninsula was Diego de Landa, a Franciscan friar who arrived there in 1549 with the intention of stamping out Maya religious practices and converting the local people to Christianity.

Landa's campaign to destroy the Maya faith and rituals reached a fevered pitch in 1562, when he launched a three-month-long inquisition. Practitioners of the traditional Maya religion were beaten, burned with hot wax, or hanged. It was recorded that approximately 4,500 people were tortured and 158 died. So horrifying were Landa's actions that Francisco de Toral, the bishop of Yucatán, reported him to the authorities in Spain and, in 1564, he was recalled to his mother country.

During the years of Landa's recall, this overzealous missionary revealed another aspect of his personality. After having burned thousands of Maya manuscripts and condemning them as containing "nothing in which there was not to be seen superstitions and lies of the devil," he settled down to write an amazingly valuable book about the Maya.

In his *Relación de las cosas de Yucatán (Account of the Affairs of Yucatan)*, Diego de Landa described in detail numerous aspects of the life and culture of the people he had oppressed, and even tried to decipher their written language. His outlining of the workings of the Maya calendar in the *Relación* and his reproduction of the Maya glyphs for the days and the months make his work the most important source of such information that existed on the eve of the Spanish conquest.

In 1572, Landa was exonerated by the Spanish authorities, elevated to the rank of bishop, and returned to Mexico to succeed Toral as the second bishop of Yucatán. Landa died in 1579. It was later discovered that some Maya codices had, by good fortune, survived Landa's wrath, having been sent to Europe by other members of the colonial administration.

Searching for More Information About the Maya

The mid-1800s explorations of John Lloyd Stephens were inevitably followed in the latter half of the century by those of a spate of eager Mayanists. Edward H. Thompson of Massachusetts arranged for an appointment as U.S. consul in Mérida, the one-time Spanish capital of Mexico's Yucatán Peninsula. Thompson had been entranced by Frederick Catherwood's twenty-one engravings of the Maya ceremonial site of Chichén Itzá, which had appeared in Stephens' *Incidents of Travel in the Yucatan.* Thompson arrived in Yucatán in 1885 and, in 1894, he purchased Chichén Itzá for $500.One particular area of interest for him was the Sacred Well, a sinkhole of greenish-black water in the limestone crust of the Yucatán plain known as a **cenote**. Thompson dredged the so-called Well of Sacrifice, into which the priests of Chichén Itzá were said to have cast precious objects and even human beings as offerings to the gods, and he eventually dove into its waters to investigate its contents.

After Thompson left Chichén Itzá in the 1920s, Sylvanus G. Morley, who was deeply interested in Maya art, hieroglyphs, and calendrics, began a twenty-year project there to record and copy some of its monuments. Throughout the 1900s, a long list of epigraphers joined Morley in the challenging task of deciphering the Maya glyphs. Today roughly 80 percent of the known glyphs have been deciphered and translated, adding enormously to our knowledge and understanding of the Maya.

Archaeologists have been aided in their examinations of Maya buildings, carvings, and artifacts by radiocarbon dating, which was developed in 1947. Carbon 14, a radioactive form of carbon, has proven useful since 1950 in determining the age of surviving organic matter, such as bones, teeth, natural fiber, and wood. For example, by burning a small sample of a carved wooden **lintel** spanning a doorway in a Maya structure, the age of the tree from which the lintel was cut can be determined. This dating technique is useful because the radioactivity in once-living things decays at a known rate that allows scientists to measure the age of organic materials up to several thousand years old.

At the opposite extreme from the up-close examination of the physical remains of Maya civilization is today's distance imaging via satellite data, known as remote sensing (RS). Through the work of a NASA archaeologist, investigators have been able to actually see from extremely high altitudes what lies beneath the tangled undergrowth of abandoned Maya cities and ceremonial sites. Old plazas, causeways, canals, and buried structures are revealed, as well as settlements with their onetime fields of maize—the basic food of the Maya—and their irrigation systems, when present.

One of the most vital elements needed to study the Maya of the Classic Period is an understanding of their food supply. The food of the Maya, sometimes referred to as their "breadbasket," not only fed the populace but supported priests, officials, nobles, rulers, and the great centers in which they lived. One of the

ongoing mysteries of the Maya is what may have happened to their food supply to bring about the collapse of so many of their vibrant and prosperous cities in A.D. 900. Remote sensing via aerial or satellite data may offer some of the answers.

Our knowledge so far of the ancient Maya comes from many sources. We have learned about the Maya from Spanish conquerors and nineteenth-century explorers, from linguists and epigraphers, from specialists on the ground, and from satellites in Earth's atmosphere, among many others. But there is still much to be learned about the shaping of their great civilization, their view of the world around them and the universe beyond, and the influences of the past on their modern descendants.

Chapter I

GROWERS OF MAIZE

The first human migrations to the Americas are believed to have taken place at least 20,000 years ago. Ice Age nomads from Asia crossed the land bridge that spanned what would later become the Bering Strait, venturing onto the new continent and dispersing to the east and the south. According to some archaeologists, the first humans to people the Americas reached the isthmus of Central America at least 13,000 years ago.

The lives of the new arrivals continued much as they had in their former homeland. They hunted the mastodons, mammoths, bison, and other large mammals of the Ice Age. But gradually the ice caps began to melt, and the sea levels began to rise. In addition to cutting off further contact via land between Asia and the Americas, these climate changes altered the lives of the hunting peoples. By about 7500 B.C., they turned to smaller game for their meat supply and supplemented their diet with roots, seeds, and grasses that resulted from a warmer climate and the growth of new vegetation.

Maize, which is popularly known as corn to Americans, was almost certainly developed from one or more of the wild grasses

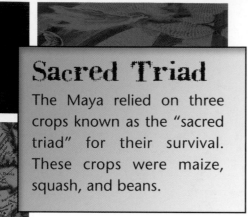

Sacred Triad

The Maya relied on three crops known as the "sacred triad" for their survival. These crops were maize, squash, and beans.

In the beginning, maize grew wild. Later, it was cultivated by the Maya and became an important part of their diet.

that thrived in the era that followed the end of the Ice Age. In present-day Mexico and Guatemala, the cultivation of the maize plant is believed to have begun around 5000 B.C.

Some historians who have studied the Maya have divided the development of their culture and the rise of their civilization into time frames that begin with an Archaic Period, lasting from about 8000 B.C. to 2000 B.C. This was a transition period during which hunting and gathering continued, while the cultivation of the domesticated grass that would evolve into maize was in a state of development. Wild animals still offered a plentiful food supply. Among the larger animals hunted were deer, a type of wild pig known as the peccary, and the gentle, long-snouted tapir, which is distantly related to the horse and the rhinoceros. Wild turkeys, rabbits, monkeys, iguanas, and the raccoonlike coati were widely available for food. The early Maya hunted predatory beasts such as the jaguar, the puma, and the ocelot mainly for their pelts.

While the roaming Maya subsisted mainly as hunters, there was no opportunity for them to develop a settled life with an assured and stable food supply. Without a reliable source of sustenance, no civilization consisting of social and political groups, of villages and even cities, could come into being. Nor would there be any way to mobilize human labor to employ the technology of the day, much less to produce the monumental architecture that became a feature of Maya sites. The numerous city-states of the Maya that gradually arose in both highland and lowland settings in present-day Mexico, Guatemala, Honduras, El Salvador, and Belize were dependent on one basic need—a guarantee of agricultural suffi-ciency. In the case of the Maya lands, as well as much of Mesoamerica, that guarantee rested mainly on the production of maize.

The Maya "Breadbasket"

By the beginning of the period known as the Preclassic (2000 B.C. to A.D. 200), early village life based on maize farming was already in place. Wherever corn could be grown with relative ease, settlements of thatched-roof dwellings surrounded by flourishing fields appeared.

The first and more difficult step toward creating settlements was clearing the land of vines and tree saplings. Only stone axes and similarly blunt tools were available. So, once the major growth was disposed of, the Maya set fire to the remaining brush. This method was known as slash-and-burn agriculture. While the woody ash fertilized the soil briefly, the soil of the Maya jungle sites, once stripped of its natural cover, was quickly depleted of its nutrients. It was soon discovered that fields could not be replanted unless they

The early Maya relied on hunting as a means of survival. A close-up image from a Maya manuscript shows a man returning from a hunt with a deer.

were allowed to lie fallow for four to seven years, when new woody growth appeared and the slash-and-burn process could be repeated. In the meantime, the Maya peasants were steadily engaged in clearing both new and older fields.

In drier or less tropical sites, like the limestone plain of the Yucatán Peninsula, new growth took longer to reestablish, and fields had to lie fallow for as many as fifteen to twenty years before they could be replanted.

Planting the corn, in contrast to clearing the land, was relatively simple. The Maya peasant made holes in the rocky, uneven soil with a dibble, a sharpened digging stick usually made of wood, and dropped in the dried corn kernels saved from the previous harvest. He depended on the jungle rains to sprout the seed. And typically, in time, he also dropped dried beans into holes beside the corn kernels. The bean vines would wind themselves around the growing corn stalks. Eventually varieties of squash, as well as chili peppers, tomatoes, sweet potatoes, and starchy roots like cassava and jicama joined the roster of Maya foods grown in the soil.

The Maya settlers also cultivated the jungle-growing breadnut tree and learned to grow avocados, papayas, and other fruits. They raised bees for honey, favoring a species that did not sting. But maize remained their agricultural staple, estimated to have made up 80 percent of their diet.

The method by which the Maya produced their everyday bread, known in Spanish as the tortilla, or "little cake," was universal among the peoples of Mesoamerica. The dried, ripened kernels of corn were scraped from the cob and soaked in a mixture of water and white lime, which was brought to a boil to soften the hulls and release the grains within. The moist grains were then rolled into a doughy mass on a flat stone, known to today's Mesoamericans as a **metate**. The corn "dough" itself, called *zacan*, was rolled out with a stone rolling pin, or **mano**. The metate and mano of the ancient Maya were often fashioned from basalt, a volcanic rock.

To prepare the tortillas for a meal, the Maya pinched off chunks of zacan, deftly shaped them into large, flat rounds, and baked them on a stone griddle over an open fire.

The tortilla could be eaten as is or could be used as a scoop for beans or vegetables seasoned with chili pepper. Zacan also lent itself to steaming rather than toasting. Wrapped in a corn husk and boiled in water, it became a cooked cereal paste. The corn husk wrapper of the Spanish-named tamale, or "bundle" was not eaten. Or, zacan could be mixed with water and boiled to make a loose porridge known as pozole. Sweetened with honey, a mixture of zacan and water became a beverage called *atole*.

A modern photograph shows some of the common Maya foods.

The Maya "Barnyard"

While hunting wild animals and birds continued through the agricultural settlement period, the Maya also began to domesticate certain animals for food. Among them were turkeys bred from the wild variety. The Maya also kept dogs. While some were used for hunting, others were fattened on corn and slaughtered for food. And, like other animals that could be brought to the altars in a living state, dogs were sometimes offered as sacrifices to appease the Maya gods.

The use of maize extended to a favorite intoxicating drink made from fermented corn and flavored with a tree bark. Known as **b'alche**, this beverage was liberally imbibed at religious festivals. It is also believed that the ancient Maya elite took b'alche enemas for purposes of intoxication, which may explain the presence of bone tubes found in the tombs of some rulers of the Classic Period.

Lives of the Maya Farmers

While the Maya priests, nobles, and rulers of the Classic Period lived in stone palaces and performed their duties from the platforms of temples and the tops of imposing pyramids, the vast majority of the population lived in huts. Their homes were made of spaced cane poles lashed together with vines and plastered with mud. Roofs, in the tropical lowlands especially, were steeply pitched to throw off rain and were covered with heavy palm thatch. Mainly rectangular but sometimes oval or square, these dwellings had packed earthen floors and were furnished with earthen pots for storing food, sleeping hammocks, and other bare necessities.

Days were spent mainly in the cornfields, which had to be

weeded regularly and watched in case rainwater accumulated in the ripening ears. To prevent the formation of mold and subsequent rot, the farmer bent each ear of corn downward as it ripened. On the other hand, rainfall might be too infrequent at times, even in the tropical lowlands. So the Maya peasants dug irrigation channels designed to flow through the cornfields. In the highlands the farmers created stone terraces on the hillsides and laboriously brought up soil from the silt-rich streams and riverbeds below.

The Maya peasants gathered many valuable natural products from the wooded areas and the waterways adjacent to their cultivated fields. Cacao beans grew on trees in the rich soils of coastal Guatemala, El Salvador, and Belize. The relative scarcity of wild-growing cacao trees made the beans so valuable that they were used as a type of currency throughout Mesoamerica. Cacao beans were also prepared as a beverage that was drunk only by the elite. Its chocolate flavor, unsweetened, was deeply bitter, and the drink was often spiced with chili pepper as well.

The sapodilla tree, which grew throughout the tropical lowlands, was the source of a hard, reddish wood used in the rooms of palaces and temples, a latex sap that yielded chicle, the main

Cacao beans were so precious to the Maya that they were used as currency. A scene from a Maya vase shows a figure grinding cacao beans into a powder or paste.

ingredient in chewing gum, and even an edible fruit. And from the copal tree came a resin known as *pom* that was used as incense in religious ceremonies.

The coastal Maya had the advantage of gathering fish, turtles, and ornamental marine shells, as well as salt from lagoons near the shore. Salt was especially important to the nutrition of a people who ate a nearly meatless diet and was an important item of trade. Fish was usually dried in order to preserve it for storing, while turtle shells and conch shells were often used as musical instruments. Turtle shells became percussion instruments when struck with antlers, and conch shells served as war trumpets.

Also from the sea, the needlelike spines of the stingray were in great demand by the Maya priests and rulers. The Maya elite, and even the common people, used the ferociously sharp spines to pierce their tongues and other body parts. The purpose of these personal bloodletting rites was to win favor with the Maya gods. Diego de Landa, describing this practice in the 1500s, wrote, "They pierced their tongues in a slanting direction from side to side and passed bits of straw through the holes with horrible suffering."

Landa also wrote in his *Relación* of 1566, "There is in this land a great quantity of medicinal plants of various properties . . . most useful and effective." The tradition of gathering medicinal plants to treat infections, burns, rashes, and internal ailments goes back to early Maya times. The healers who prescribed their use were known as **h'men**, doctor-priests who sought spiritual as well as physical cures for their patients.

Narcotic drugs derived from plants were also artfully used to stun fish in dammed sections of streams and lakes. So powerful were the substances that the Maya added to the water that the fish rose to the surface in a stupor and could be picked out by hand.

Maya Garments and Adornment

Cotton, which was grown in the Yucatán and at Maya settlement sites elsewhere was the basic material used for clothing. Henequen, or sisal, a much coarser natural fiber, was used for making ropes, fishing nets, and carrying bags. The common garment of the Maya peasant was a loincloth, a long strip of cotton known as an *ex* that could be wound around the waist and passed between the legs. Most peasants went barefoot, the soles of their feet thickened from childhood to withstand rough terrain studded with stones and thorns.

Maya women wore a cotton skirt or a simple square-cut shift that hung from the shoulders, known as a *huipil.* Both sexes covered their shoulders with a capelike square of cotton, or perhaps animal skin, known as a *pati* that was also useful as a blanket.

With the advent of the Classic Period of Maya civilization, starting around A.D. 200, society became more stratified, and a powerful elite arose at such Maya sites as Copán in Honduras, Tikal in Guatemala, and Palenque in Mexico. The clothing, jewelry, and personal adornment of priests, nobles, and rulers became elaborate and lavish beyond anything the peasants and other working people of the Preclassic Period had ever known. But as the general wealth of the Maya city-states increased, the populace aspired to imitate those aspects of adornment they could afford.

The Maya elite favored elaborate headdresses and wore garments woven with patterns of exquisite

A sculpture shows a woman wearing a huipil, a traditional Maya dress.

Jade Stones and Quetzal Plumes

To the dismay of the Spanish conquerors of the Maya lands, there was no gold or silver to be found. But the ancient Maya did not miss these natural resources. The hard green stone, often with bluish highlights, known as jade could be found in highland streams and fashioned, with painstaking difficulty because of the lack of metal tools, into magnificent jewelry, ornaments, and figurines. Maya rulers were often buried with quantities of jade adorning their bodies and, in time, their tombs were broken into to obtain this precious commodity.

Even rarer than jade, and thus highly favored by the Maya rulers, were the feathers of the quetzal, a bird native to the highland cloud forests of Guatemala, Honduras, and the Mexican state of Chiapas. The iridescent green-gold tail feathers of the quetzal, as much as 3 feet (1 meter) in length, were fashioned into the elaborate headdresses of the most powerful rulers, while the lesser nobility had to make do with the feathers of such jungle birds as the macaw and the toucan.

detail, dyed in rich colors derived from plants, or interleaved with the colorful feathers of macaws, hummingbirds, and the **quetzal** bird. The skins of jaguars, ocelots, pumas, and other fierce animals were reserved for people of the highest rank and were used as garments, capes, and sandals. The Maya rulers wore large, heavy earplugs of bone, shell, or jade, as well as nose and lip ornaments. Massive pendants hung from their necks. Their bodies were decorated with tattoos and paint, and they filed their front teeth into points or zigzag patterns and inlaid the outer surfaces with mosaics of jade.

The hallmark of Maya beauty was a prominent nose and a sloping forehead. Crossed eyes, too, were considered an asset. Among both the upper classes and the ordinary people of the Maya city-states, it was the custom to bind the heads of newborns and to flatten their foreheads between boards. A dangling bead suspended above the head of an infant caused the eyes to focus inward. While the peasants and workers of ancient Maya society are seldom depicted, carvings and paintings of kings, queens, and other prominent individuals show ample evidence of these acquired physical characteristics.

The Maya people also imitated the elite in tattooing their faces and bodies and in the wearing of nose, ear, and lip jewelry fashioned from wood, bone, and shells. Earlobes that were pierced in childhood were filled with wooden plugs.

But even more important than kingly style and fashion in the daily lives of the Maya were the religious precepts and rituals practiced by their rulers and dictated by their priesthood. For vital to the growers of maize, as well as to Maya civilization itself, was the favor of the gods.

The gods of the Maya were seen to be primarily responsible for the sun, rain, and soil that would continue to guarantee an

A Maya figure is depicted with earflares, a type of ear ornament. The figure was found at Copán.

adequate food supply. But this was not all. Every other aspect of life, from birth to death, depended on the beneficence of the gods. To understand natural phenomena, to find auspicious dates on the calendar, to predict the future, and to interpret the human relationship with the divine, Maya of all classes turned to powerful religious leaders. For it was only these authorities who could predict the future by reading the stars, explain the mystery of time, and help the people by guiding their destinies.

Chapter II

GODS AND PRIESTS

The *Popol Vuh*, which came to us in the post-conquest 1500s via the Quiché Maya of Guatemala, describes the creation of the earth, the heavens, and the Underworld, as viewed by the Maya of ancient times. This valuable document also relates how the creator gods fashioned the first humans. In the first creation, the gods populated the earth with animals. But the animals could not speak, so the gods tried to mold humans out of clay. The clay humans were limp, though, and the rains melted them. In their third attempt, the gods tried to make humans out of wood, but the rains drowned them. Finally, the gods created humans from maize, using the corn paste, zacan, for their flesh and water for their blood. The truth that lies within the fourth and successful Maya creation myth points to the very early presence of corn as the staple of Maya life.

The Maya universe is described as follows. The earth, or Middleworld, is square and flat, resting on the back of a huge turtlelike or crocodilelike creature. The four cardinal directions are associated with colors. The east is red, the place of the rising sun. The south is yellow and seen as the right hand of the sun. The north is white, for it has to do with those ancestors

The Hero Twins are shown here on a painted vase with their father.

who have died. The west is black, for it is associated with death itself and the Underworld. A giant tree stands at the center of the Middleworld, its roots reaching down into the dreaded Underworld and its lofty branches reaching to the longed-for Upperworld.

A major portion of the *Popol Vuh* is taken up with the evil gods of the Underworld, a place also known as Xibalba, and the Hero Twins, who outwit them in a long series of adventures. The victory of the Hero Twins over the forces of cold and darkness was seen by the ancient Maya as a way for humanity to achieve the hoped-for afterlife rather than having to spend eternity in the "Place of Fright."

A Look at the Maya Gods
The Maya gods, who presumably dwelled in the Upperworld, were assigned various functions that sometimes overlapped, as did their names. They varied in appearance, too, for some gods

One of the Many Adventures of the Hero Twins

The Hero Twins, named Hunapu and Xbalanque, play the game of infuriating and overpowering the Lords of Death of Xibalba, not with brute strength but with mischief and cunning. During their stay in the Underworld, the twins annoy the gods by engaging, night after night, in the traditional Maya ball game, which is played on a court with a rubber ball. At last the gods become so angry that they substitute Hunapu's head for the ball. But the quick-thinking Xbalanque saves the life of his hapless brother by turning his severed head into a rabbit that bounds away. The evil lords are so distracted by this trick that Xbalanque has time to restore Hunapu's head to his body, and both twins survive.

Defeating the Lords of Death was of special importance to the Maya rulers because of their divine status and their hope that they would experience an afterlife as celestial beings. As a result, their burial attire and their tombs would contain the imagery necessary for overcoming the gods of the Underworld.

were depicted in human form and others as animals or phenomena of nature, and even these images were subject to change.

Among the more standard members of the Maya pantheon was Itzamnaaj. He was seen as the supreme god, the creator of humankind, the inventor of writing, and the patron of learning. When portrayed in human form, Itzamnaaj was depicted as a toothless old man with a prominent nose. Unlike some of his fellow deities, Itzamnaaj was always benevolent.

His wife was Ix Chel, the goddess of childbirth, healing, weaving, and the moon. But, oddly, this nurturing-seeming goddess

Itzamnaaj is considered to be the supreme god in the Maya religion. This sculpture depicts the god as an old man.

was portrayed in human form as wearing a headdress of snakes that were entangled in her hair and as having toes and fingers that resembled jaguar claws. Ix Chel was feared as well as cherished because of her ability to cause floods and destruction. Many of the other gods were the descendants of Itzamnaaj and Ix Chel.

Among them were Huun Ixim, the maize god, a young man from whose head sprouted an ear of corn, and Chaak, the rain god. The latter was both friendly and terrifying, for although he brought the much-needed moisture for successful farming, he was also the instrument of storms, thunder and lightning, and even war and human sacrifice. Accordingly, the human image of Chaak was that of a man with a curling snout and the fangs of a reptile.

The sun god, known as K'inich Ajaw or sun-faced lord, traveled across the sky by day. But at night he was believed to sink beneath the earth into the Underworld, where he became the fearful Jaguar God. Among the gods portrayed as human, the death god, Ah Puch, was the most gruesome, for he had a skeletal nose, jaw, and spinal column, and his body was covered with hideous spots.

Numerous other gods with specific duties existed in the Maya pantheon. They served as patrons of bee-keeping and of the calendar; of merchants, traders, and cacao bean growers; of hunting and fishing; of poetry and music.

Religious rituals among the farmers, workers, and other commoners of the ancient Maya were surely seen as a source of security. Priests or other religious officials were almost certainly consulted as part of commoners' everyday lives, from birth to adolescence, from marriage to death. There were also public festivals keyed to special dates on the Maya calendar and to occasions such as pleas for agricultural bounty, for the health of a new ruler, and the success of a military campaign.

To gain the favor of the gods, religious rituals and festivals were preceded by acts of self-denial with regard to food (no meat or savory flavors such as chili peppers or salt), abstinence from sex, and even self-mutilation on the part of the populace. Tongues, lips, ears, cheeks, and male organs might be pierced to offer human blood to the gods before the crowds poured into the ceremonial sites, colorful and noisy with banners and with processions that were accompanied by the sounds of drums and trumpets.

Evidence of bloodletting among the ancient Maya is most clearly documented in the carved stone lintels, ceramic figurines, and polychrome pottery of the Classic Period that depict rulers and nobles, the elite of the Maya world, performing such acts. For, as those closest to the divine, the Maya kings had the most to lose if they lost favor with the gods. Their enduring power as heads of state, their success in overcoming

A mask panel shows the face of K'inich Ajaw, the sun god.

their enemies in warfare, and their entry into the Upperworld when they died were all at stake.

Personal Bloodletting and Human Sacrifice

Mayanists of the first half of the 1900s, such as Sylvanus Morley and the British archaeologist J. Eric S. Thompson, viewed the ancient Maya as a gentle, peace-loving people who dedicated their lives to prayer and to searching the heavens for knowledge and spiritual guidance.

Morley and Thompson believed that the peasantry of the Classic Period subsisted, as in much earlier times, on crops produced through slash-and-burn agriculture, and that they lived in small settlements at some distance from the temple sites. Modest and devout priest-kings who did not seek personal grandeur oversaw the ceremonial centers. Writing in 1946, Morley stated that, "The Maya inscriptions treat primarily of chronology, astronomy . . . they are in no sense records of personal glorification and self-laudation like the inscriptions of Egypt."

What then of the Well of Sacrifice at Chichén Itzá on the Yucatán Peninsula? Morley and Thompson explained the evidence of human sacrifice among the Yucatán Maya as resulting from the Postclassic invasions of the fierce and bloodthirsty Toltecs of central Mexico, who themselves later fell victim to the Aztecs.

With the gradual decipherment of the Maya glyphs beginning in the 1960s, however, it became clear that the rulers of the Maya in major Classic Period sites such as Copán, Tikal, and Palenque were very much interested in increasing their power and prestige. Not only were the great lords almost constantly engaged in warfare with neighboring city-states, but one of the main purposes of battle was the taking of captives that would be publicly sacrificed to the Maya gods. And the precursor to such major undertakings as warfare was the letting of the blood of the great lords themselves, as well as that of their ladies.

Most striking among many examples of personal bloodletting rites seen in Maya art are three carved stone lintels taken from a structure at the ancient Maya site of Yaxchilán in the Mexican state of Chiapas. In the first panel, known as Lintel 24 and dated October 28, 709, we see Shield Jaguar, the powerful warrior king who ruled Yaxchilán from A.D. 681 to 742, standing over his principal wife, Lady K'ab'al Xook, holding an enormous torch. Both figures are magnificently adorned in elegantly patterned clothing. Shield Jaguar's elaborate headdress includes the shrunken head of a human victim. He wears jade ornaments and jaguar-skin sandals.

In Lintel 24, Shield Jaguar stands with a flaming torch while his wife Lady K'ab'al Xook performs a bloodletting ritual. The Maya believed that bloodletting was a way for them to offer tribute to their gods.

Lady K'ab'al Xook, kneeling at her husband's feet, is drawing a thorn-studded rope through her tongue in an act of bloodletting to honor and sustain the gods. The rope falls into a basket, which contains bark paper stained with drops of blood. Lady K'ab'al Xook's expressionless face may be the result of a state of shock induced by the intense pain and considerable blood loss caused by this form of self-mutilation.

In Lintel 25, which bears the earlier date of Shield Jaguar's accession to the throne, October 23, 681, Lady K'ab'al Xook is also seen kneeling following a bloodletting rite. Alone on this panel,

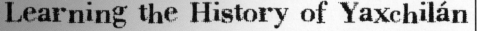

Learning the History of Yaxchilán

Yaxchilán is located in a lowland jungle site on the Usumacinta River, which divides present-day Mexico and Guatemala. It was a flourishing trade center and a major city-state of the Classic Period. Through the work of accomplished epigraphers, such as the Russian-born Tatiana Proskouriakoff, we have learned a great deal about the dynastic history of Yaxchilán, from its first ruler in the A.D. 300s, through its apex in the late 600s and the 700s, to its demise in the 800s.

The mystery of the abandon-ment of Yaxchilán, along with that of so many of its neighbor-ing cities, remains unsolved. When the British Mayanist Alfred Maudslay first came upon the site in the late 1800s, it was concealed by tropical forest, many of its structures crumbling and its inscriptions of dates and rulers indecipherable. It took until the early 1960s to learn Yaxchilán's true history, for it was then that Tatiana Proskouri-akoff was able to, as she put it, "pry open a chink in the wall of obscurity."

she has burned the bark paper onto which her blood has fallen and gazes upward at the rising smoke from which a hallucinatory snake, known as a Vision Serpent, emerges. In Lintel 26, Shield Jaguar again appears with Lady K'ab'al Xook. He is dressed for battle in cotton armor studded with stones, and Lady K'ab'al Xook, blood still oozing from her tongue, hands him his shield and his jaguar helmet. One objective of Shield Jaguar's warfare may have been the taking of captives for human sacrifice. The Maya kings, having derived their absolute authority from the gods, were required to maintain a cycle of blood offerings in order to retain their power.

Shield Jaguar's son, Bird Jaguar, who came to the throne in 752, ten years after the death of his father, also ordered a series of carved lintels at Yaxchilán dealing with bloodletting and hallucinatory visions of the gods in the form of serpents. They are identified as Lintels 15, 16, and 17. Lintel 17 celebrates the birth of Bird Jaguar's son and heir, elsewhere given as February 18, 752. His second wife, not the mother of the child, is seen drawing a rope through her tongue, while Bird Jaguar makes ready to pierce himself with an awl of sharpened bone. Stingray spines were also

Lady K'ab'al Xook experiences visions as a result of bloodletting in Lintel 25.

used as lancets for this purpose. There are many clay figurines and polychrome pottery paintings that illustrate, with spurting drops of blood, this bloodletting rite among the Maya male elite.

Diego de Landa, writing in the 1500s, described human sacrifice just prior to the Spanish conquest, as the local people of the Yucatán had portrayed it to him. Further evidence of the brutal practices at Chichén Itzá was to be found in the gruesome carvings on its stone structures of human skulls and of jaguars devouring the hearts of victims.

Landa wrote that the Maya first painted the body of the intended victim blue, the color of sacrifice, and then lay him on his back on a stone atop the temple platform. Four old men, known as *chaaks*, after Chaak, the god of rain and human sacrifice, also painted blue, each held him by an arm or leg.

"At this time," Landa continued, "the executioner, the **nacom**, with a knife of stone, and with much skill and cruelty struck him with the knife between the ribs of his left side under the nipple . . . plunged his hand in there and seized the heart." According to Landa, the executioner placed the still-throbbing heart on a plate and gave it to a priest who anointed the faces of the idols with the fresh blood.

Some accounts of the human sacrifices of pre-conquest times indicated that the corpse was then hurled from the top of the temple platform to be disposed of by the spectators. Arrow sacrifices were also said to have taken place. The victim, painted blue, was tied to a stake and shot with arrows directed at the heart by the executioners, to the point at which the living organ could be removed using the traditional knife of sharpened stone or **obsidian**. Victims who were tossed into the Well of Sacrifice at Chichén Itzá, however, might presumably escape death if, once beneath the water, they were granted the favor of the gods. Slaves, cap-

A mural in a room at Bonampak shows warriors with captives who will be used for sacrifices.

tured enemies, criminals, and children, especially orphans or off-spring of unknown parentage, were among those most frequently chosen for human sacrifice.

In spite of the belief of the early Mayanists that human sacrifice was practiced exclusively during the Postclassic and pre-conquest periods, there is now much evidence that the great rulers of the Classic Period went to war largely for the purpose of securing sacrificial victims. This was particularly true after the A.D. 600s. Nor did the kings of the warring city-states execute their captives readily. Often they put them on display and inflicted torture on a prolonged basis. Wall paintings, pottery vessels, ceramic figurines, and stone carvings show prisoners being dragged by the hair, scalped, forced to let blood, having their fingernails torn out or the tips of their fingers severed, and even disemboweled before being bound to a scaffold to have their hearts ripped from their bodies.

The Calendar and the Cosmos

Little is known of the lives of the individual members of the priest-hood and other religious leaders of the Classic Period, with the exception of the great rulers themselves. Yet it would appear that officials of a fairly high calling were required to interpret the wills of the gods who demanded the rites of bloodletting and human sacrifice. Likewise, priests or similar religious figures were almost certainly charged with interpreting the phenomena of nature as seen through the movements of the planets and the stars, of keeping the complicated Maya calendar, and of designating the most auspicious dates for both private and public undertakings.

The ancient Maya were possessed of remarkable mathematical skills, which they used to make the complex architectural calculations required to build their cities and to mark time and thus record historical events. Calendrics were also important for determining when to schedule ceremonial events and when to expect the movements of the various celestial bodies that might affect such events and undertakings.

The Maya observation of the solar year resulted in a 365-day calendar, similar to the one that is most familiar to us, which they called the **Haab'**—sometimes referred to as the Vague Year because it was about six hours short of a true solar year. Unlike our Gregorian calendar, the Haab' did not add an extra day every fourth year as we do in leap years.

Also, unlike our calendar, the Haab' was divided into eighteen months of twenty days each. As these divisions multiplied to only 360 days, the Maya tacked on five additional days at the end of

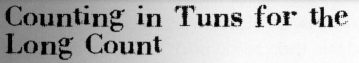

Counting in Tuns for the Long Count

The Maya counted by 20s rather than 10s because they used all their fingers and toes as the basis of figuring, rather than just their fingers. As a result we call their number system vigesimal as opposed to ours, which is a decimal system. To count elapsed time, the Maya used a unit of time of 360 days, which was called a *tun*. The tun, when divided by the number 20, was made up of 18 units, which were known as *winals*. Each winal consisted of 20 *k'ins*, or days.

Going in the direction of larger units was the *k'atun*. It consisted of 20 tuns, or 7,200 days. Next came the *b'aktun*, which contained 20 k'atuns, or 144,000 days. The *pictun* was equal to 20 b'ak'tuns, or 2,880,000 days. Continuing with *kalab'tuns*, *k'inchultuns*, and additional multiples of 20, the ancient Maya had no difficulty in measuring time in terms of millions and billions of days.

K'atun endings were a time of important public and religious ceremonies, for they marked the close of twenty 360-day periods, and each k'atun had its own patron deity. Some Classic Period sites held observances at the close of ten 360-day periods as well. These 3,600-day units were known as *lajun-tuns*. The main event marking a time-period ending such as a k'atun or a lajun-tun was the building and dedication of a monument inscribed with the date and with some historical information.

the year to bring the total to 365. Each month had its own name glyph, as did the added five-day period known as Wayeb', which was thought to be an unlucky time of year. This calendar was used for civic purposes, such as to mark the reigns of the Maya kings and other governmental matters.

The Maya also kept a sacred calendar of 260 days that was linked to their personal lives, marking birth dates and yearly rituals based on their relationship to the gods. Known as the **Tzolk'in,** this 260-day Sacred Round was not divided into months but consisted of thirteen numbered days and twenty named days. This system offered 260 different combinations so that no two days in the Tzolk'in shared the same number and name. Each one had its own meaning and its own symbol.

While the Haab' and the Tzolk'in were independent of each other, they also ran simultaneously, meshing like interlocking cogwheels and producing what was known as the Calendar Round, a 52-year period of 365 days each. Multiplying 365 by 52 yields a total of 18,980 consecutive days in the lives of the ancient Maya that were unique in their naming and in their significance.

For calculating really long periods of time and probably to legitimatize the Maya rulers as having been descended from the gods, the Maya devised a calendar known as the Long Count. The beginning of time on the Long Count calendar corresponds to August 13, 3114 B.C. on our calendar. On that date, the Maya believed, the gods created the world of their time. Nor was it the only time the earth had been created, for Maya belief held that there were and always would be cycles in which the world was created, destroyed, and created again.

In view of the mathematical, calendric, and observational skills of the Maya, it is not surprising that they were so involved with the cosmos. Their astronomical observatories were limited to the architectural pinnacles of their structures. Their observations were surely hampered in the rainy lowlands by many nights of cloud and mist throughout the year. Their measuring instruments, too, were limited, for they probably charted the positions of celestial bodies by means of crossed sticks set into fixed positions. Yet they

It is believed that this building was used by the Maya to observe the skies.

were able to calculate the cycles of the moon, lunar and solar eclipses, the movements of Venus, and to a lesser extent those of Mercury, Mars, Saturn, and Jupiter.

In addition to constructing many of their temples, palaces, and public buildings to be in alignment with various phenomena of the skies, the ancient Maya used their knowledge of astronomy to make prophecies and to predict the future. For the Maya rulers in particular, the behavior of the celestial bodies was the key to timing many important events in their lives. Included among them were ceremonies of accession to the throne, the presentation of an heir, the onset of battle with a neighboring city-state, as well as the rituals of bloodletting and of offering sacrifices to the gods.

Chapter III

RULERS OF TIKAL AND PALENQUE

The Maya city-states of the Classic Period (A.D. 200 to 900) were ruled by a series of all-powerful kings. Their authority, which they believed had been derived from the gods, was passed on to their eldest sons who, in turn, took their place as divine rulers. Women, too, sometimes reigned over the Maya city-states. But the Maya queens were generally placed in the highest office only when it was feared that the dynasty faced extinction.

Despite their absolute power over populous kingdoms of architectural distinction, of which there were about sixty during the Classic Period, no one ruler ever managed to unify the city-states of the Maya world. Occasionally a powerful state gained temporary control over a neighboring one. But for the most part, the individual kings fought for their autonomy, and a balance was achieved through frequent warfare.

From their carved portraits, we have learned about great rulers and their heirs, as well as their forebears, and about their deeds and the major events of their lives. Some of these portraits appeared even before the onset of the Classic Period. During the Late Preclassic era, between 100 B.C. and A.D. 100, there were already established cities in the Maya area. Among them was Kaminaljuyú, in the highlands of Guatemala, its present-day site almost overrun by the sprawl of Guatemala City. From the site has been salvaged the remarkable stone pillar known as Stela 25. The carving on this stela depicts a ruler wearing the mask of Itzamnaaj, the supreme god and the creator of humankind.

Although Kaminaljuyú, which once had temples, marketplaces, and canal networks, now consists of approximately two hundred mounds, findings at the site have included pottery, jewelry, and tools, as well as an excavated tomb in which a ruler had been laid to rest with jade finery and human sacrificial victims.

This "Place of the Ancient Ones," according to the translation of Kaminaljuyú, was in due course abandoned, as were other sites in the temperate Guatemalan highlands, mainly, it appears, in exchange for sites in the jungle lowlands, where the Classic Period of Maya civilization burst into splendor. The decision of the Maya to build their great cities in the lush but tangled rain forests may have reflected their need for a more abundant food supply, but it has never been fully explained.

Tikal, Pyramids in the Petén

In the heart of the tropical lowland region of Guatemala, known as the Petén, lay the Classic Period

This stela is one of the many discoveries found at Kaminaljuyú.

Rulers, Nobles, Commoners, and Slaves

The Maya lords ruled over a highly ordered society that was divided into clearly defined classes. Just below the divinely endowed king were the aristocrats and nobles, many of whom were his close relatives. They included top civil administrators and military officials, chief overseers of trade and of the distribution of food supplies, and the highest-ranked scribes and members of the priesthood.

Lower-ranked scribes, priests, and administrative officials made up a subsidiary class. Among them were also found architects, engineers, master craftspeople, merchants, professional warriors, and large landholders.

Next came the commoners, which included small farmers, serfs who worked on the large estates, laborers, craft workers, and domestic servants. Lastly, there were slaves, commoners who had fallen into poverty, and criminals and prisoners of war who were of too lowly a status to be considered suitable for human sacrifice.

The courtly life of the Maya rulers had its own rituals, pomp, and pleasures. In attendance in the palaces were the wives of the kings, for most seemed to have more than one, as well as jesters, dwarves, and musicians. Only on great public holidays, in celebration of special events, did the commoners upon whose labor the entire structure of the kingdom was based have an opportunity to glimpse the nobility and possibly even the ruler himself.

city-state of Tikal. It is believed that its towering ruins were encountered by westerners for the first time in 1695, when a Spanish priest and his companions became lost in the swamps, sweltering heat, and thorny shrubbery of the Petén jungle.

Although the early fortunes of this extensive kingdom rose and fell due to invasions and strife with neighbors, Tikal emerged triumphant in the late A.D. 600s. From then until the late 800s, when the demise of the Classic Period sites began, it boasted a thriving population of 60,000 and some of the most impressive temple-pyramids ever built. Its Great Plaza was flanked on the east and west by two of its six tallest structures, the highest one, Temple IV, ascending to 229 feet (70 m). Elsewhere lay other platform temples, palaces with plastered rooms, and stelae, all richly carved and embellished, as well as broad causeways, ball courts, and evidences of the thatched-roof huts of Tikal's food growers and laborers.

Tikal's ruling dynasty may be traceable to the A.D. 100s in late Preclassic times, but the first dated monument identifying a ruler appeared in A.D. 292. The names of the Maya rulers are often confusing. Some were based on the names of the gods, of nature, of animals, or of supernatural creatures or phenomena. Epigraphers have identified others by a number or letter, while many have nicknames derived from the actual appearance of their glyphs. Nicknames are used because some of the names have yet to be deciphered. Also, the dates of their reigns are often approximate rather than exact and uniformly agreed upon.

The colorfully named Jaguar Paw I—also known as Chak Tok' Ich'aak I, and alternately nicknamed "Great Burning Claw"— ruled from A.D. 359 or 360 to around 378. This Tikal king has been portrayed on carved stelae, in ceramic figurines, and on incised pottery, adorned with jewels and a royal headdress. On a

At Tikal, Temple IV is the tallest structure in the Great Plaza.

stela carved in 376, he is shown trampling a bound captive. Jaguar Paw I was highly successful in his establishment of trade routes, including remarkably long-distance ones with the city of Teotihuacán in Mexico, near the present-day site of Mexico City.

There is also evidence that, in A.D. 378, Teotihuacán made aggressive forays into the Maya region, killing Jaguar Paw I and installing its own kings in Tikal and elsewhere. Examinations of skeletal remains indicate that the new rulers were of non-Maya stock.

Throughout the A.D. 400s, Tikal continued to be ruled by dynastic kings, possibly of Central Mexican origin and from war-like Teotihuacán. Among them were the ruler nicknamed Curl

Nose, his son Stormy Sky, and finally Jaguar Paw II, who died in 508. The first female ruler to appear on a stela at Tikal was probably the wife of Jaguar Paw II and the mother of his successor Double Bird. Dubbed Lady of Tikal, she ruled from around 508 to possibly 527, but never completely in her own right. Nor were the A.D. 500s and 600s a time of growth for Tikal. Trade and other relations with Teotihuacán appear to have come to a halt due to the demise of that center, reducing Tikal's economic prosperity.

Calakmul, Kingdom of the Snake

Calakmul, which lies deep in the rain forest of the Mexican state of Campeche, was discovered in 1931. It was in badly eroded condition because of the chalky quality of the local limestone used in its construction and the intensity of the tropical rainfall. Investigations of the site, begun in 1984 and still in progress, point to its having covered more than 11 square miles (30 square kilometers), nearly twice the area of Tikal. Calakmul had more than six thousand structures, including numerous palaces and 115 stelae, more than any other Maya site.

Calakmul's emblem glyph, the symbol of its dynasty, is believed to be a snake head. Prominent among its kings, other than Yuknoom the Great, were Scroll Serpent, who ruled from 579 to 611 and who attacked the rich tropical site of Palenque—an amazing 150 miles (250 km) away in the Mexican state of Chiapas—in both 599 and 611. Calakmul experienced its golden age in the 600s and, like other lowland Maya kingdoms, met its demise in the late 800s.

For 130 years, from A.D. 562 to 692, no dated monuments were erected. At the same time, Tikal came into conflict with its neighbor and rival power to the north, Calakmul.

In 657, Calakmul's ruler, Yuknoom the Great, or Yuknoom Ch'een II (who had come to the throne in 636) attacked Tikal in a struggle that was to engage him until his death in 686. As two of the largest lowland sites, the two superpowers had long been in competition for supremacy and had forged numerous alliances with smaller powers in an attempt to overcome one another. It was not until the accession in 682 of the Tikal ruler Jasaw Chan K'awiil I—also referred to as Ruler A—that the fortunes of Tikal revived. A great building program was begun, and Tikal regained its prominence in the Petén.

The occasion of Jasaw Chan K'awiil I's defeat of Calakmul was recorded on an intricately carved lintel of sapodilla wood placed high in the ceiling of Temple I on the Great Plaza of Tikal. The carving is dated August 5, 695, and states that Jasaw Chan K'awiil "brought down the flint and shield" of the Calakmul king, Yuknoom Xich'aak K'ak', or "Fiery Shield."

The reign of Jasaw Chan K'awiil I lasted for fifty-two years, from 682 to 734. On his death he was buried in Temple I, also known as the Temple of the Giant Jaguar. This pyramid, which is crowned with an intricately decorated roof comb, rises to a height of 154 feet (47 m). When Jasaw Chan K'awiil I's tomb was opened in 1960, it revealed the king's skeleton and a trove of riches. His body had been

Jasaw Chan K'awiil I, also known as Ah Cacau, was buried in the Temple of the Giant Jaguar. This vessel was one of the objects placed in the tomb.

placed on a funerary stone bench and was adorned with magnificent jade, pearl, and shell jewelry. Among the grave offerings in his tomb were vessels of jade, mosaic, and painted ceramic and an amazing collection of bone objects delicately incised with tiny glyphs and scenes of fishing and travel in dugout canoes.

Tikal continued to prosper during the A.D. 700s under the descendants of Jasaw Chan K'awiil I. But as the great city-state entered the A.D. 800s, its building projects slowed, and its population started to decrease. Its dynastic line had been crumbling, and the last stela appears to have been erected in 869. Soon the thatched houses of the diminished population of farmers and laborers sprang up among the great monuments of the ceremonial plazas. Squatters took over the once-forbidden palaces and temples of the elite. And, with a little more time, the encroaching jungle moved in, smothering with avid vines and saplings the city that once had been.

The reason for Tikal's collapse, which was shared by all of its lowland neighbors and signaled the close of the Classic Period by the early 900s, has never been fully explained. But there are a number of theories, and the causes may very well be multiple.

Were the lowland sites abandoned because of overpopulation and an inadequate food supply due to a prolonged drought or other natural disasters such as earthquakes or hurricanes? Was there a foreign invasion, an epidemic of disease, or a severe decline in trade? Or did the populace lose faith in the divine powers of their rulers and rebel against their excessive demands for labor, tribute, and soldiering?

In their pursuit of glory and self-acclaim, the Maya kings tended to record only positive achievements. Few stelae were carved after the A.D. 800s, and those that have been found offer no clues as to the reasons for the imminent demise of the city-states.

Nor has any funerary pottery told the story of the Classic Period decline. Codices written on bark paper, textiles such as painted curtains or wall hangings, and other fragile materials disintegrated long ago in the hot, damp climate of the lowland jungles.

Palenque and the Tomb of Pakal

Although the ancient Maya city-state of Palenque is sometimes described as a "highland" site, its elevation is little more than 1,000 feet (305 m) above sea level, and its partially mapped area of habitation lies in a tropical rain forest in the Mexican state of Chiapas. Amid tangled greenery alive with the sounds of macaws and howler monkeys lie the major structures of Palenque. Built of fine-grained sandstone embellished with exquisite carving, they include a vast palace with a four-story tower that had open court-yards and long vaulted galleries. Palenque's Temple of the Sun is an exquisite, small pyramid-temple with an elaborately carved mansard roof and a tall roof comb.

Almost no stelae have been found at Palenque. But their absence is more than made up for by the famed Temple of the Inscriptions in which was discovered, in 1949, the secret entry to the most impressive of all Maya burial sites, the tomb of the great ruler K'inich Janaab' Pakal.

K'inich, or "sun-faced," Pakal came to the throne of Palenque in A.D. 615 as a twelve-year-old boy. The early rulers of the Palenque dynasty can be traced back to the A.D. 400s and included the first queen known to have ruled with full power among the Maya kingdoms. She was Lady Yohl Ik'nal, the sister or the daughter of the previous king, who had left no heir, and the grandmother of Pakal. During the rule of Lady Ik'nal, which lasted from 583 to 604, Palenque underwent, in 599, the first of two major assaults by the aggressive Scroll Serpent of Calakmul.

A wall carving of K'inich Pakal was discovered at Palenque, which is located in Chiapas, Mexico.

The second assault took place in 611 during the reign of her son, who was succeeded by another queen, Lady Sak K'uk', the mother of Pakal, from 612 to 615. The sacking of Palenque by Calakmul in 611 is recorded in hieroglyphic text on the Temple of the Inscriptions. It reads "Palenque was axed."

Although the rule of Pakal the Great extended from 615 to 683 and he died at the age of eighty, he is better known for his burial site and the rich contents of his tomb than for his achievements. His long reign, however, is believed to have been a relatively peaceful one.

During a restoration of the inner sanctuary of the Temple of the Inscriptions in the 1940s, the Mexican archaeologist Alberto

Ruz Lhuillier noticed that on the floor of the temple that topped the pyramid were stone slabs, one of which had a double row of holes in it. Clearly the holes, when unplugged, were designed to be a means of lifting the slab.

On doing so, Ruz and his workmen discovered a shaft packed with rubble that appeared to lead down toward the base of the 65-foot-tall (19.8 m) pyramid. It took four seasons to remove the tightly packed rock-and-stone fill, revealing that the shaft contained a stairway, which changed direction about halfway down.

When at last, in 1952, Ruz and his excavators reached the bottom of the staircase, they entered a short corridor containing the skeletons of five or six young adults who were probably human sacrifices. The far end of the chamber was blocked with a huge triangular slab of stone, a sealed doorway. With the removal of the slab, Ruz entered the remarkable funerary crypt of Pakal the Great.

"Out of the dim shadows," Ruz wrote, "emerged a vision from a fairytale. . . . Across the walls marched stucco figures in low relief. Then my eyes sought the floor. This was almost entirely filled with a great carved stone slab in perfect condition. . . . Ours were the first eyes that had gazed on it in more than a thousand years!"

The burial chamber itself was 30 (9 m) by 13 feet (4 m) and 23 feet (7 m) high. The carved slab that filled most of the chamber proved to be the cover of a limestone sarcophagus in which lay the king's skeleton, teeth and bones tinged bright red with cinnabar, a mercury compound much favored in the royal burials of the Maya. The king's remains were adorned with rings, bracelets, breastplates, and earplugs of jade, and his face was covered with a mask of jade mosaic in his own image, the eyes fashioned from bits of shell and obsidian.

The relief carving on Pakal's sarcophagus lid depicts the king falling from the Middleworld. Below him lies the perilous Underworld and above him the Upperworld to which, as a divine ruler favored by the gods, he will surely ascend. As was the custom, a jade bead had been placed in Pakal's mouth as an offering to ease his passage into the afterlife.

K'inich Kan B'alam, Pakal's son, was already forty-eight years of age when he ascended the throne. His reign, from 684 to 702, was taken up with the completion of his father's tomb, including hieroglyphic texts and carvings in stucco and stone of gods and ancestors. Kan B'alam's own life-size portrait in stucco plaster, which once adorned the roof ornamentation of one of his temples, is remarkably realistic. It gives us a striking picture of a Maya lord, with sloped forehead, elongated nose, and out-thrust lower lip. Kan B'alam added three temples at Palenque, known as the "cross group" and including the Temple of the Sun. These structures, dedicated in 692, blended Maya myth and history in intricately carved texts and pictures of great beauty and complexity.

The A.D. 700s appear to have brought Palenque into increased conflict with the rival kingdom of Toniná, 40 miles (64.5 km) to the south on the higher Chiapas slopes. Most prominent among the dynastic rulers of Palenque in this era may have been K'inich

This jade mask is believed to be of Pakal the Great. It was discovered in his burial chamber.

Ahkal Mo' Naab' II, who acceded to the throne in 721. Excavations begun in the late 1990s and still ongoing, have yielded a tomb in Palenque's jungle-draped South Acropolis decorated with painted murals, the first of its kind found on this site. The tomb also contains a tall support pier bearing a sculpture believed to be a likeness of K'inich Ahkal Mo' Naab', as well as a throne inscribed with more than two hundred glyphs.

The last known ruler of Palenque before its collapse came to the throne in A.D. 799. Although he was named Janaab' Pakal III after his gloriously buried ancestor Pakal the Great, almost nothing is known of his reign or his fate.

Chapter IV

RULERS OF COPÁN, CARACOL, AND CHICHÉN ITZÁ

"Architecture, sculpture, painting, all the arts which embellish life," John Lloyd Stephens wrote in 1841 following his 1839 visit to Copán, "had flourished in this overgrown forest." Now, however, "All was mystery; dark, impenetrable mystery."

The ruined site that Stephens and Catherwood explored in the lush uplands of Honduras, at an altitude of some 2,000 feet (610 m), were visited again in the 1880s by the English Mayanist Alfred Maudslay. But the difficulties of travel to the area and of finding a labor source to help with investigations of the Copán monuments persisted. Yet no scholar of the Maya could give up on this remote ceremonial center.

Its stelae were outstanding because they were so deeply incised and were carved in such high relief that the figures on them were sculpted almost in the round. Also, they bore more hieroglyphic inscriptions than stelae at any other Maya site. Nor could the investigators of Copán cease to wonder at the

Temple of the Hieroglyphic Stairway, the risers of its 63 steps—33 feet (10 m) wide—carved with 2,200 hieroglyphs.

The reading of the glyphs, which were in time found to be a portion of a dynastic text, did, however, pose difficulties. This was due to the poor quality of the limestone in the Copán area. Rubble fill for the site's pyramids and temples was held together with mud rather than limestone mortar, as at some other sites. As a result, the upper halves of the temples tended to collapse. Nor did the local limestone supply plastering mortar of the quality required for floors and exterior surfaces.

The Copán site did have some agricultural advantages. Its soil was rich and well watered for the growing of crops, and sources of both jade and obsidian were to be found in the immediate vicinity. K'inich Yax K'uk' Mo' is thought to have been the founder of the Classic Period Copán dynasty, having ruled from 426 to 437. His tomb, which was not discovered until 1996–1997, was found in a deeply buried, early temple platform.

Although the tomb was small in size, the ruler was suitably adorned in a collection of jade ornaments, his front teeth were inlaid with jade, and his bones were coated red with cinnabar. The skeleton of Yax K'uk' Mo' also showed a variety of bone injuries probably obtained in hand-to-hand battle, including a broken right arm. A similarly damaged limb appears in a portrait of the monarch that was carved in stone.

Of Copán's seventeen rulers, the first eleven kings were often identified by number rather than by name, and sometimes by both. But we can view the sixteen principal rulers of Copán on the famous four-sided Altar Q, constructed at the base of a pyramid-temple in 776. Along with their name glyphs, the rulers (four on each side of the altar, starting with Yax K'uk' Mo') are portrayed in carved stone. We do not, however, get a fuller

The steps of the Temple of the Hieroglyphic Stairway are covered with more than two thousand hicroglyphs.

Altar Q has given us the identities of the sixteen principal rulers of Copán. Their names and portraits are featured on the sides of the altar.

picture of these rulers until we come to the reign of Smoke Imix God K, or Ruler 12, during Copán's great era, as a result of Copán's many broken monuments.

Smoke Imix took the throne in 628 and, as Copán's longest-ruling king, died in 695. He is believed to have been about fifteen when he ascended the throne, later embarking on an extensive building program. His successor, Copán's Ruler 13, did not have so fortunate a reign. Waxaklajuun Ub'aah K'awiil, also known as 18 Rabbit, who came to the throne in 695 and ruled during the height of Copán's artistic achievement, suffered a dire end when, in 738, he was captured in battle and beheaded by Cauac Sky,

Quiriguá, Challenger of Copán

Quiriguá was a relatively small city-state that lay 30 miles (48 km) north of Copán in Guatemala, just across the present-day border with Honduras. For some time, possibly as early as the 400s, it had been under the control of Copán, probably because of its strategic location on the river trade route between the Honduras uplands and the Caribbean coast.

By the 700s, however, Quiriguá's fortunes had improved and, with the accession of Cauac Sky in 724, found itself ready to throw off the overlordship of Copán. Details of the battle and the decapitation of 18 Rabbit are not clear. But the disgraceful death of Copán's ruler resulted in a do-nothing, caretaker government under 18 Rabbit's successor, known as Smoke Monkey, who ruled from 738 to 749.

Quiriguá, in the meantime, took over control of the profitable trade route on which it sat.

Although it never approached Copán in size, it began to build magnificent monuments. Quiriguá's stelae, the tallest ever erected by the Maya, were inscribed on all sides, deeply incised, and elaborately sculpted almost in the round in the style of Copán. On the base of one of them, Cauac Sky boasts of the power he attained "in the land of Ruler 13" by means of his great victory. And on the monuments of Quiriguá's Great Plaza he makes five references to the decapitation of 18 Rabbit, whose emblem glyph he adds to his own titles.

Cauac Sky, who ruled for more than sixty years, died in 785. Two Quiriguá rulers, Sky Xul and Jade Sky, succeeded him, the latter taking the throne in 797. The last known date inscribed at Quiriguá reads 810. Shortly thereafter, the site entered its last phase, and its ceremonial center became deserted.

the ruler of the neighboring city-state of Quiriguá. No more disgraceful death for a Maya king could have been anticipated. Would the Copán dynasty and the great kingdom itself ever recover from such a blow?

The Revival of Copán's Fortunes

At Copán, the humiliation of the beheading of its ruler 18 Rabbit was not recorded for many years. When the king's demise was finally referred to, there was no mention of his capture and decapitation. He was said to have died in battle by "flint and shield."

With the death in 749 of 18 Rabbit's inept successor, Smoke Monkey or Ruler 14, came the ascent of Ruler 15, known as Smoke Shell. Smoke Shell's ambition was to reclaim the former glory of Copán, and he did so through the construction of the Temple of the Hieroglyphic Stairway, the lower portion of which had been commissioned by 18 Rabbit.

When completed, the stairway was embellished with six life-size sculptures of former kings of Copán. At its base on a free-standing pillar known as Stela M stood a carving of Smoke Shell. The declared purpose of the structure was to honor the glorious rule of Smoke Imix, or Ruler 12. But it was also probably intended to erase the memory of the ignoble death of 18 Rabbit.

The dynastic history written in the stairway's 2,200 glyphs is the longest known Maya inscription. An investigation of the temple stairway begun in the 1890s revealed a jumble of collapsed blocks of stone that had to be carefully analyzed and reconstructed in keeping with the text. The complete restoration of the temple stairway was of such magnitude that it continued well into the closing decades of the 1900s.

Copán's dynastic Ruler 16 was Yax Pasaj Chan Yoaat. He was crowned in 763, while still a boy of about nine, and reigned possibly until 820. Among his major achievements, prior to the beginning of Copán's collapse, was the construction of Altar Q, which portrayed his fifteen royal predecessors and himself—sixteen stone figures in all. In a crypt close to Altar Q, Yax Pasaj entombed the bodies of fifteen jaguars, snared and sacrificed at what must have been great human risk in honor of his royal ancestors.

Ukit Took', the seventeenth and final ruler of Copán, ascended the throne in 822. By this time, the site is believed to have been suffering from food shortages, deforestation, infant mortality, and disease and depopulation among both peasants and the elite classes.

During its apex, Copán may have incorporated a population of 20,000. However, as in the case of the other Maya sites of the Classic Period, it appears to have become the victim of its own success. In the years immediately following Copán's demise, remnants of the peasantry moved into the center and hauled stones from the great ceremonial structures to use as platforms on which to build their thatch-roofed houses.

The Amazing Metropolis of Caracol

At an altitude of just under 3,000 feet (914 m) in the lush rain forest of present-day western Belize lies the remarkable Maya city-state of Caracol. Its ruins were first reported in 1937 by a timber gatherer, and for many years Caracol was thought to have been a moderately small

Stela M shows Smoke Shell, the fifteenth ruler of Copán.

Tombs for the "Middle Class"

As far as is known, commoners among the ancient Maya were customarily buried beneath the dirt floors of their thatch-roofed houses, accompanied by a few personal goods and, in their mouths, a little food and a jade bead to appease the gods of the Underworld.

A surprising find at Caracol was the existence of masonry tombs in relatively simple residential complexes. Some appear to have been family tombs, containing the remains of more than one individual. But all were provided with grave goods that included objects of jade, obsidian, and exotic shells. Some of the skeletal remains of nonelite residents of Caracol exhibited teeth inlaid with mosaics of jade.

Even more surprising was the presence in the relatively humble masonry tombs of small ceramic pots containing human finger bones. It is believed that it was a ritual to amputate fingers from the hands of both living adults and children to deposit in the graves of family members as offerings to the dead. It is hoped that relatives were not required to contribute more than one digit per burial to the pottery caches—one vessel contained twenty-two finger bones—that were common in the household tombs of the lower social orders of Caracol.

kingdom with little political clout among its powerful neighbors, which included Tikal and Calakmul.

Intensive investigations beginning in 1983, however, revealed a very different story. In the late Preclassic Period, during the A.D. 100s, Caracol had built an impressive monument consisting of a massive platform crowned with three pyramids, as well as a number of palaces that must have served religious, administrative, and residential purposes. Richly appointed tombs, too, were found in

An aerial photograph provides an unusual view of the main temple at Caracol. From this vantage point, it is possible to get a sense of the structure's enormous size.

this early complex, which the Maya called Sky House and which has been named Caana.

Even more unusual information about Caracol came to light. With an estimated population of 60,000 to 80,000 people at its peak, the city had a huge number of outlying residential districts reached via a network of paved roads known as *sacbés*. The roads, which radiated from the ceremonial center like spokes in a wheel, were built of mounded rubble smoothed with limestone plaster.

The outlying dwelling areas were themselves densely settled, and their farmlands, which were made up of raised stone terraces, were highly productive. Nor were the inhabitants of Caracol's suburbia of as lowly an order socially and economically as those at other Maya sites. In some ways, in fact, their lives—and especially their deaths—could be compared with those of the elite rulers of the kingdom.

Back at the seat of government in the ceremonial center of Caracol, with its large plazas, pyramids, palaces, and ball courts, the dynasty in power could be traced to A.D. 331. Its founder was Te' K'ab' Chaak, or "Tree Branch Rain God." But in the early days of the Classic Period, Caracol appears to have been a client state of Tikal, which lay to the northwest. As late as the 500s, its kings may have acceded to the throne under the patronage of rulers from Tikal. This was the case in 553 at the enthronement of Caracol's Yajaw Te' K'inich II who, in 562, delivered a telling attack on Tikal and formed an alliance with its enemy and rival power, Calakmul.

The peak years for Caracol, which began in 562, included the forty-year rule of K'an II, a son of Yajaw Te' K'inich II by one of his younger wives, from 618 to 658. It was during this period of prosperity and expansion that a broad segment of the city-state's non-elite inhabitants began to share some of the wealth and privileges of their overlords. This phenomenon does not appear to have occurred in any other Classic Period Maya city-state.

A setback for Caracol seems to have taken place during the 700s, probably due to a decline in the fortunes of its ally Calakmul. In any case, for the 118 years between 680 and 798, major construction did not go forward. Caracol's fortunes revived briefly in the early 800s, only eventually to go the way of the other Classic sites. Caracol's last ruler is known simply as Ruler XIII, and its last glyph is dated 859.

Chichén Itzá, a Postclassic City

"The opening of the wells of the Itzá" is the English translation of the name of this Maya site, which is located on the limestone plateau of the Yucatán Peninsula of present-day Mexico. The wells of Chichén Itzá and neighboring Postclassic sites are natural formations in the broken crust of the earth that have filled up with water from underground streams, producing deep ponds known as cenotes. Best known among those at Chichén Itzá is the large

At Chichén Itzá, the Maya would make offerings to their gods by tossing objects and human sacrifices into a well.

Sacred Cenote, or Well of Sacrifice, into which both precious objects and human beings were thrown as offerings to the gods. While the reference to the wells at this Maya site is easily explained, some mystery remains regarding the origin of the word *Itzá*. According to the Maya writings in the *Books of Chilam B'alam*, the Itzá were a "foreign" people who reached the Yucatán sometime during the 900s and who "speak our language brokenly." Most authorities tend to agree that the Itzá may have come from the Gulf Coast state of Tabasco in Mexico along with the so-called Putun Maya, both arriving by sea in large canoes. Perhaps they were one and the same people. And perhaps they were allied with another Mexican people, the Toltecs, from the faraway city of Tula, north of present-day Mexico City.

In any case, Chichén Itzá, the origins of which may possibly date back to the A.D. 600s, became by the 900s a very different-looking Maya city from the lowland and other Classic Period sites that were abandoned in the 800s.

The Life and Death of Chichén Itzá

Unlike the rulers of the Maya sites of the Classic Period, those of Chichén Itzá—which dominated the Yucatán from A.D. 1000 until its demise in the early 1200s—left almost no historical information about their dynastic history, the dates of their accessions, and the great events of their reigns. It has been suggested that Chichén Itzá was ruled by councils of lords, priests, and warriors in a variety of groupings, and that the carved and painted portraits found on the site's monuments are of just such individuals rather than a single ruler who held supreme power.

The monuments and relics of Chichén Itzá show evidence of Maya and Toltec cultural hybridization. Hammered gold disks recovered from the Sacred Cenote tell us about what may have

Kukulcán, or the Feathered Serpent

Kukulcán is the Maya language translation of Quetzalcoátl, the god of non-Maya Mexican peoples who was portrayed as a large, fanged snake with the feathered body of a bird. Stone carvings of this creature had never appeared at sites built by the Classic Period Maya. But at temples in Chichén Itzá from the Postclassic, we are introduced to this fierce creature. In pairs of columns, we see its scaly head resting at the base of tall supporting pillars carved with layers of long feathers.

Chaak, the both benevolent and threatening rain god long known to the Maya, appears at Chichén Itzá but in a Toltec form known as a **Chacmool**. Gone is the sloped, pointed skull and elongated nose along with the elaborate headdresses of the old Maya gods and kings. The Chacmool at Chichén Itzá reclines at the top of a temple stairway. He has small, even features and wears a "pillbox" hat. He lies with knees raised, holding a receptacle for offerings with his head turned outward toward the plaza.

Skull racks, or long, carved stone friezes of the heads of human skeletons on stakes, can also be attributed to the Toltecs, as can the snarling jaguars and those seen devouring human hearts in the relief panels of Chichén Itzá.

The Ball Game of the Ancient Maya

Relief sculptures at the base of the Great Ball Court at Chichén Itzá portray a victorious ball player who has decapitated his losing foe. This and similar scenes indicating that the game was played to the death were interpreted by scholars like Sylvanus Morley, who began his work at Chichén Itzá in 1924, as resulting from the influence of the warlike Toltecs. But the later examination of painted ceramics, pottery figurines, and stone carvings from the Maya Classic Period prove that the game was traditionally one that was played either to the death or for the purpose of obtaining victims deemed worthy of human sacrifice.

The number of players on the opposing teams varied widely, from perhaps as few as one or two to eleven. The courts, too, varied in size and in pattern of construction. Some had one or more stone rings placed high on the walls, indicating that the object was to send the heavy rubber ball, weighing 5 pounds (1.9 kilograms) or more, through them. Other courts had no rings, and perhaps the sloping sides played a role in the scoring.

In any case, the object of the game appears to have been for the players to score goal points without using their hands or feet. Only upper arms, shoulders, waists, hips, and thighs could be used to strike the ball. As a result, players wore thick padding around their waists and pads that protected their elbows and knees.

The Mesoamerican ball game was still being played at the time of the Spanish conquest among descendants of the Aztecs, the Maya, and others. The ball at that time was about 8 inches (20 centimeters) in diameter, and the stakes were often valuable possessions rather than death. Spectators placed bets, and when goals were scored by the opposing team, they fled the viewing stands to prevent the seizure of their jewelry, clothing, and other belongings.

been a fierce initial struggle for Toltec inroads. A Toltec warrior is seen spearing a traditional Maya soldier. And the very presence of gold at Chichén Itzá speaks of its having been brought from sources in the distant Valley of Mexico.

Chichén Itzá's Temple of the Warriors features the feathered serpent columns and the reclining Chaak figure of the Toltecs. And the four-sided pyramid known as El Castillo is dedicated to the god Kukulcan. Do its nine stories, however, represent the nine Lords of Xibalba, the Maya Underworld? And what of the round temple at Chichén Itzá that surmounts a series of platforms and is known, because of its snail shape, as the Caracol (not to be confused with the Classic Period Maya site of that name in Belize)? Does the fact that the Caracol's stone window openings point to positions on the horizon where Venus rises indicate that it was a traditional Maya observatory blended into a Toltec-inspired structure?

Lastly, Chichén Itzá had at least thirteen ball courts, including the largest one in Mesoamerica, which measures approximately 490 feet (149 m) in length and has sloping walls that are roughly 27 feet (8.2 m) high. Ball courts have been found at almost all Maya sites of the Classic Period, and it is believed that the game was derived from one of the many mythical exploits of the Hero Twins and their victory over the Gods of the Underworld. Yet, the ball game was played elsewhere in Mesoamerica among non-Maya peoples from very early times. So both the true origin of the intriguing and often deadly ball game, as well as the rules by which it was played, remain mysteries to this day.

Some time in the early 1200s, possibly around 1221, it appears that Chichén Itzá was sacked, perhaps by the small rising state of Mayapán, 62 miles (100 km) to the west on the Yucatán Peninsula. It is believed that the rulers of Mayapán, who were of a family known as the Kokoom, brought in mercenaries from Tabasco to reduce Chichén Itzá to ruin and abandonment.

Mayapán, however, was a pale shadow of Chichén Itzá in terms of both size and architectural prominence. As the last of the major cities to dominate the Yucatán in the Postclassic Period, it met its end in 1441. Only a scattering of petty states futilely attempting to gain power over one another were to be found in the region at the time of the Spanish conquest.

Chapter V

SCRIBES AND ARTISTS

Without the scribes and artists of the ancient Maya, we would not have been able to identify the dynastic rulers of the Classic Period, read their written history, or have knowledge of the calendars that influenced the great rulers' activities and undertakings. Nor would we have the visual evidence of the kings' sculpted monuments and of their artifacts of pottery, jade, bone, and wood.

Yet relatively little is known about the lives of the scribes and artists who are responsible for our widespread and steadily advancing knowledge of the society they recorded. Like almost all professions and occupations in the Maya hierarchy, however, scribes and artists had their own patron gods, either in the form of twin monkeys or a single "monkey man."

A striking example of a monkey scribe god is that of a stone figurine found at Copán. He has a human face, with wide facial planes, a broad nose, and small eyes, that bears no resemblance to the typical sloped forehead and elongated nose of the Classic Maya. Sitting in a crouch on his knees, the monkey god is seen holding in his left hand an ink pot fashioned from a sectioned conch shell. In his right hand, he holds a paintbrush. The ear of a deer, placed just above his small monkey ear, further identifies this deity.

Scribes were members of the highest level of Maya society. Some are believed to have been the brothers or sons of kings, and their position was very likely hereditary. Others may have functioned as both kings and scribes, and there is evidence of scribal tombs, indicating that they ranked with the great rulers as candidates for everlasting life in the Upperworld.

In the royal palace the scribe was a close adviser to the ruler, for he kept the calendar, made astronomical calculations, and announced the most auspicious times for accessions to the throne, royal marriages, and embarking on warfare with neighboring city-states. At schools for scribes, the highest-ranking officials in that category taught those of lesser rank the elements of mathematics and writing that were required for their profession. Nor were the Maya scribes limited to number skills and writing. Many painted and created intricate works of art as well.

Many scribes were related to royalty and often played an important supporting role to the ruler.

Unscrambling the Maya Glyphs

Efforts to decipher the Maya script began with Diego de Landa in the mid-1500s. Landa was able to identify and record the Maya name glyphs for the eighteen months plus the five-day unlucky period of the 365-day Maya calendar, and the name glyphs for the twenty days of each month. He also attempted to coordinate the Maya glyphs with an alphabet based

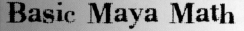

Basic Maya Math

Neither the counting of cacao beans for the purpose of barter nor the complicated calculations of the Maya calendar system could have been accomplished without a basic means of counting. Maya arithmetic was simple to the degree that it involved just three symbols—a dot (which stood for the number 1), a bar (for the number 5), and a shell (indicating a zero).

As a result, numbers 2 to 4 were represented by groups of horizontally arranged dots. Number 5 was a single horizontal bar. Number 6 was a bar with a dot just above it. Number 7 was a bar with two dots above it, and so on through number 9.

Number 10 was written as two horizontal bars, one directly above the other, and dots above

the double bars took care of numbers 11 to 14. Number 15 consisted of three bars, one atop the other, and numbers 16 through 19 utilized dots above the bars.

Continuing this system would have been increasingly clumsy, so the Maya developed a vertically rising positioning arrangement, whereby values increased in multiples of twenty. Here the shells, or zeros, came into play. They were used as substitutions for the basic numbers (1 through 19) in order to raise their values to the next higher multiple on the position chart, as necessary. The easiest way to understand the Maya numbers beyond 19 is to read them from the bottom up on a chart where both the numbers and their multiples are indicated.

on the phonetic sounds of Spanish. But the Maya writing system that Landa encountered, which probably had its origins in at least 200 B.C., was far more complex than he imagined.

Today we know that Maya glyphs are of three basic types. Some are logographs, or word signs, representing a complete word or a group of words. Others are phonetic signs, representing the sound of a syllable and usually made up of a consonant plus a vowel. Yet other glyphs are semantic signs, signs that specify the meaning of the main glyph in a block of glyphic symbols. Both phonetic glyphs and semantic signs can be thought of as "helpers" that give range and variation to the basic written message.

The list of epigraphers who tried to decipher Maya writing is long, and their findings were made through trial and error. Translations in the 1800s were hampered for many years by a mistake in how the glyphs should be read. The correct way for most glyphs to be read was from left to right and from top to bottom.

Prominent among the epigraphers of the 1950s was the Russian Yuri Knorosov. Although Knorosov was not allowed to leave the Soviet Union, he did highly valuable work on the phonetic approach to the reading of Maya glyphs. An important breakthrough on the meaning of the Maya glyphs—other than giving us numerical and calendrical information—was the discovery of the German-Mexican Heinrich Berlin, in 1958, that certain types of glyphs were unique to certain sites. These so-called "emblem glyphs" told us the names of the ancient city-states and provided clues as to the political structure and organization of the Classic Period.

Even more information became available through the work of Tatiana Proskouriakoff starting in the 1960s when she realized that the inscriptions contained historical narratives or biographical information about the Maya rulers. Proskouriakoff's "event glyphs" tell us about births, marriages, deaths, accessions, wars, and sacrifices to the gods.

How much writing could the average member of Maya society read? It is possible that ruler names, day and month names, and bar-and-dot numbers were recognizable to most of the

Inside the Blocks of Glyphs

Most Maya writing is presented in the form of columns or grids containing blocks of glyphs. How are any of the 1,100 or so known Maya glyphs arranged in each individual block, and what is the order for reading both the individual blocks and the grids?

Usually there is a main glyph plus added symbols that clarify the meaning. The so-called "affixes" to the main element in the glyph may reinforce its meaning, vary it, or even change it to something quite different. An example of a word that can be spelled as a logograph and as a syllabic spelling is the name of the great ruler of Palenque, Pakal. In his name glyph the main ele-ment is a portrayal of a shield, which in the Mayan language is the word *pakal*. Accompanying the main element are three phonetic signs that read, from top to bottom, *pa, ka, la*. As the final vowel in the final syllable is not pronounced, the phonetic signs also present us with the name Pakal.

The normal reading order both within a glyph block and in a text is from left to right and from top to bottom. There are, however, a number of variations and complications, especially when texts consist of many columns or appear in L-shapes, circles, or in other inscription patterns.

nonelite inhabitants of the city-states. Traders and military lead-ers, too, needed to have a degree of literacy in order to relate to the neighboring city-states that they visited on missions of peace and war. But, for the most part, it is almost certain that literacy was confined to the ranks of the elite classes—the rulers and their closest administrators and advisers, and especially the profes-sional scribes of the Maya city-states.

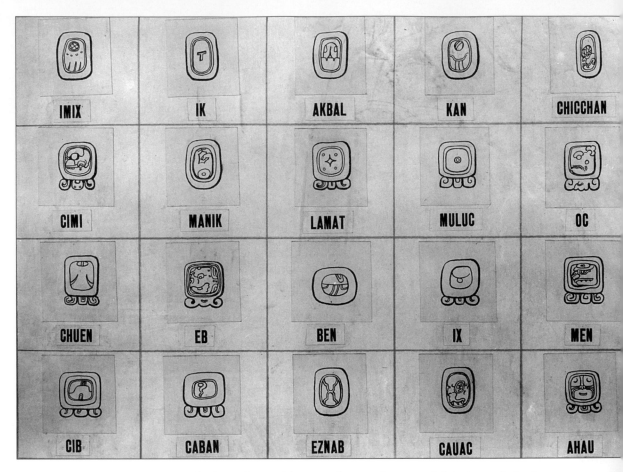

Commoners might have been able to understand some of the signs of the Maya language. This modern illustration shows the pictograms for the days of the year.

Architecture of the Maya

Very little is known about the lives of the laborers who built the great stone monuments and other structures of the Maya ceremonial and administrative centers. Neither writings nor pictorial media tell us about them or about the methods they used in the building of cities, chiefly for the purpose of glorifying their kings.

We do know, however, that huge work forces must have been required to clear and level forest and jungle sites of trees and undergrowth, to quarry blocks of limestone, and to convey them to the location chosen for the building. Although the ancient Maya did have the concept of the wheel, for they produced small toys with wheels, they had no draft animals to pull wheeled vehicles. Also their forested terrain was poorly suited for using wheeled vehicles. Log rollers were used to transport blocks of limestone, and ropes of heavy fibers such as henequen served to both lash and raise the blocks.

The cores of the temple-pyramids, the raised platforms, and the great palaces were mixtures of earth and rubble. Slabs of limestone were then cut and shaped for the exteriors using sharpened flint-stone chisels and wooden mallets. Limestone was relatively easy to work with when it was first quarried and hardened over time through exposure to the air. Limestone could also be burned to a powder and mixed with water to make a lime-based plaster that was used as mortar between the dressed stones, as a coating for stone walls and roads, as well as stucco to adorn facades and roof combs with relief carvings.

In addition to the laborers and overseers who were responsible for the actual construction of the buildings, the ancient Maya utilized the services of architects, planning engineers, toolmakers, and artists and artisans. Priests, too, were involved to select the most favorable calendar dates for the inauguration of the monuments.

Temples crowned with ornate roof combs atop tall pyramid platforms were only one of the many kinds of structures built by Maya laborers. Some but not all of the pyramids contained the tombs of great rulers, which further complicated the building process.

Palaces that served both residential and administrative purposes made up another major category of Maya structures. Often they were elongated buildings with courtyards, long galleries,

The corbeled arch is one of the best known features of Maya architecture.

and many rooms. The separate chambers opened into one another by means of the "false," or corbeled, arch, for the Maya did not know how to construct the true arch of the ancient Romans (with its wedge-shaped central keystone supporting the curve of the other stones).

Maya builders created the corbeled arch by layering stones inward until they overlapped to form an inverted V. The top of the arch was then bridged with a single, flat, horizontal stone. As a result the arches in Maya palaces and other structures were narrow and constricted. They were also weaker than the Roman arch.

Stelae and altars, as well as plazas, causeways, and ball courts, were some of the other projects of the Maya builders. The Maya called their stelae *te'-tun*, or "stone trees," for these pillars resembled trees thrust upward from the earth. Likewise, their squat altars, which could be square or rounded, were called "throne stones." Both of these freestanding memorials were heavily sculpted on almost every available surface.

Maya Artists and Artisans

Sculptors and painters carried out the interior decoration of the great monuments, including decorations on lintels and wall panels. Painting lent itself to smaller objects as well, such as bowls, plates, and vases of pottery, and ceramic figurines. The Maya did not have the potter's wheel, so vessels, whether they were intended to be either utilitarian or decorative were shaped by hand from lumps of clay, and baked over a bed of charcoal.

Maya colors were derived from plant and mineral sources, and they included a wide range of reds, yellows and tans, greens and blacks, and a blue. Most building exteriors were painted red.

The Maya artists, of whose lives we know very little, were bound by the traditions of their culture. Yet they managed to

A modern illustration imagines how a Maya artisan would work on a stela. These stone pillars were often used to record noble events.

express a remarkable range of stylistic interpretations, and the refinement of their execution was a testament to their skills. Sculptors and painters worked with shell and bone, they carved jade, stone, and obsidian, and they created polychrome pottery and a variety of fanciful figurines. Much of their effort went into the creation of funerary objects for the tombs of the Maya rulers—objects of carved and polished jade, polychrome clay pottery, and ceramic figurines especially.

There were also many products made by Maya artists and artisans that were of too perishable a nature to survive. They included the richly woven clothing of the Maya elite, featherwork derived from the quetzal and other birds, painted and engraved leather goods, and items of cotton, henequen, palm, reed, and tree bark. Only a little engraved wood, such as the carved lintels in some of the Maya temples, has survived the ravages of climate and time.

The Painted Walls of Bonampak

The most vivid and informative wall paintings produced by the Maya are those that were found at the small site of Bonampak, located some 18 miles (30 km) south of Yaxchilán, in the present-day Mexican state of Chiapas. Reports of the existence of these murals first came from Giles Healey, who was led there in 1946 by Mexican *chicleros*, gatherers of chicle from the sapodilla tree.

In a relatively small structure among buildings surrounding the main plaza, Healey came across three rooms decorated with colored murals depicting scenes from the reign of a Bonampak ruler, Chaan Muwaan, dating from A.D. 790. Due to deposits of limestone caused by water seepage, the painted murals, which wrapped around the vaulted walls of each chamber, were remarkably well preserved.

Moreover, the Bonampak murals tell us a connected story and reveal numerous details of life at court. They show us royal ceremonies and entertainments, the treatment of war captives when they came before a Maya king, and scenes of bloodletting among members of the royal family. The naturalism and detailed images of Bonampak played a role in revealing that the early Mayanists

One of the walls of Room 1 shows the infant heir being held in the arms of an attendant.

had been mistaken in their belief that the Maya were a peaceful people ruled by benevolent priest-kings.

In the murals in Room 1, we see preparations in the palace for what appears to be the presentation of an heir, the son of Chaan Muwaan. Room 2 contains battle scenes and the presentation of the prisoners of war to Chaan Muwaan. On the steps of what is presumably a temple, victims beg for mercy or lie at the feet of the king, suffering the tortures of having had their fingernails pulled out, or possibly the tips of their fingers cut off. Droplets of blood are seen falling to the ground. Another victim appears already to have been killed and to have had his heart torn out, and a decapitated head rests nearby.

The murals of Room 3 show us more scenes of pomp and ceremony, as well as members of the royal family seated on a dais, on which women in white robes draw ropes through their tongues in an act of personal bloodletting.

The details of clothing of the elite, including quetzal-feather headdresses and jaguar-skin capes, tunics, and footgear, contrast sharply with the stripped bodies of the captives depicted in the Room 2 murals. And the elaborate costumes of the parading celebrants in Rooms 1 and 3 reveal the elegance of the courtiers and the musicians at even a small Maya site such as Bonampak.

The Music of the Maya

We have no way of knowing what the music of the ancient Maya sounded like. But in the murals at Bonampak, we see several examples of the instruments they played—rattles made from dried gourds, wooden drums, and the shells of turtles. Other Maya instruments included trumpets made from conch shells, flutes fashioned from reeds, whistles made from the bones of small animals, and bells made from ceramic beads.

Occasions of all sorts appear to have called for musical accompaniment—public festivals, religious ceremonies, royal funerals, and the onset of battle. The last was almost certainly intended to frighten the enemy with the blare of trumpets and the ominous beating of drums.

Chapter VI

WARRIORS AND TRADERS

Warfare and trade were the two principal means of contact among neighboring sites during the Classic Period (A.D. 200–900) of Maya civilization. By the seventh century A.D., warfare grew increasingly prevalent. While the Maya city-states may sometimes have gone to war to secure trade advantages, the main purpose appears to have been the taking of elite captives for human sacrifice. Only in that way could the honor and power of a royal leader be perpetuated. For if a ruler failed to offer valuable sacrifices to the gods, he would lose both godly favor and the regard of his subjects.

The Maya warriors were of all ranks. They included lords, nobles, and other members of the elite, including the king himself, as well as foot soldiers of the lower orders. The latter prepared for battle by painting their bodies red and black and wore cuirasses, or breastplates, of thickly quilted cotton or tapir hide. Their weapons were wooden clubs, slingshots for hurling rocks, and spears tipped with flint or obsidian. Their elite leaders were adorned with jaguar pelts and quetzal plumes.

High-ranking priests and scribes who served as advisers to the king usually chose the time for the onset of battle. A battle may have been timed to coincide with the position of Venus,

The Glyphs of War

Carvings in stone, pottery art, and paintings, such as the murals of Bonampak, tell us about warfare among the Maya and about the treatment of captured prisoners who, if they were of sufficiently high rank, would become sacrificial victims. Once it became possible to read the writing of the Maya, it was learned that there were "capture" glyphs, signs followed by the name of the ruler who was the captor, which added to his glory. Such glyphs also gave the name of the captive and, if more than one, the count. For example, a glyph of the ruler Bird Jaguar of Yaxchilán, who came to the throne in 752, was inscribed to read "he of the 20 captives."

Glyphs for war in general also existed. The war sign included a pair of falling droplets on either side of the glyph and could be made specific by adding the emblem glyph of the city-state of the enemy to read "war against Tikal," or whoever the rival of the day might be.

the ending or onset of a calendar period, or some other astronomical factor. Public and religious rituals preceded the campaign. Warfare may sometimes have begun stealthily. But more often it was announced to the enemy with drumbeats, the shrilling of trumpets, and violent war cries.

Merchants and Traders

Ek' Chuah was the name of the patron deity of the traders and merchants who kept the Maya economy running through the distribution of both utilitarian and luxury items. He is portrayed as a black-painted god with a pack on his back in which he carried his merchandise. Ek' Chuah's people included those who trekked long distances between cities as well as those who offered goods for sale in local markets. Ek' Chuah was also the patron of cacao beans, which were used as currency among the Maya.

Long-distance traders traveled by road or jungle trail as well as by water, via streams and rivers or coastal sea routes. Frequently it was necessary to combine both modes of travel, for many sites had no direct access to water. Mainly, goods were conveyed by caravans on foot, each man wearing a tumpline—a sling across his forehead or chest—that secured his burden to his back.

The need for traders arose from the fact that no one Maya site had all of the natural resources that were required for daily life. A vast network came to be established. The trade in luxury goods, in particular, resulted from the demands of the rulers and the elite and was executed under the direct supervision of high-ranking members of the court.

Among the most wanted goods were jade from the northern highlands, jaguar pelts from the tropical lowlands, quetzal feathers from the highland cloud forests, and marine shells and stingray spines from the coastal regions. Cinnabar from iron ore, found in the southern highlands, yielded the red pigment used on the bodies of the deceased in royal burials. And cacao beans, which were in demand everywhere, grew mainly in the lowlands of the Caribbean and Pacific coasts.

Shells from merchants and traders were often used in jewelry. This is an earflare found at Copán made from a shell and features a carving of a ruler.

Everyday Articles of Trade

The economy of the Classic Maya involved the exchange of many items intended for everyday use. Some, such as pottery, basketry, textiles,

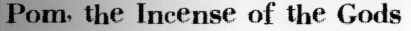

Pom, the Incense of the Gods

The resin of the copal tree, which grew in the tropical lowlands, provided the incense known as pom. There is evidence of its widespread use during the Classic Period, for remnants of it have been found in incense burners inside the ruined temples of the major sites. As a result, we know that it was used in religious ceremonies and was an important article of trade.

Diego de Landa reported on the use of pom among the Maya at the time of the Spanish conquest. The resin was formed into small cakes that were painted blue, the color of sacrifice, and decorated with cross-hatching. The cakes were then burned in pottery vessels that bore an image of the god whose favor was being sought. Cakes of pom were also tossed into the Sacred Cenote at Chichén Itzá and were sometimes molded into the shape of a heart, human or animal.

It is believed that the Classic Maya, in making their offerings of human victims to the gods, also included in their ceremonies the burning of pom, the symbolic substance of sacrifice.

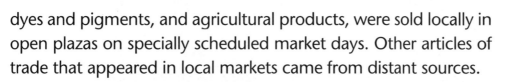

dyes and pigments, and agricultural products, were sold locally in open plazas on specially scheduled market days. Other articles of trade that appeared in local markets came from distant sources.

Salt was a necessity, especially for a people who ate a diet low in meat. Salt beds along the Yucatán coast were a major source of this product, which could also be obtained from certain inland mineral springs.

Flint and chert were stones of steely hardness that could be sharpened to serve as household cutting tools and as stone axes for felling trees and clearing land. Like limestone, the basic building

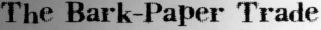

The Bark-Paper Trade

The papery bark of various species of fig trees that grew on the Pacific Coast and in some other lowland areas was an important item of trade among the Maya. Bark paper was essential for the production of the Maya books, or codices. It was also used for garments, especially costumes worn in public ceremonies. And it was burned in bloodletting rites, for the blood-spattered bark paper, once set alight, was believed to produce hallucinatory visions offering godly approval of the blood offering.

To produce the paper for a codex, the Maya pounded the tree-bark peelings to a pulp, bonded them with plant gums, and then beat them into long, flat sheets with oblong stone tools. The resulting strips of paper were folded back and forth like an accordian and coated with white lime to create a smooth finish that could be inked or painted with glyphs and illustrations. Because of its use in codices and bloodletting rites, bark paper might be considered a material of the elite. But it was also an article of everyday trade because the work of so many artisans was required for its production.

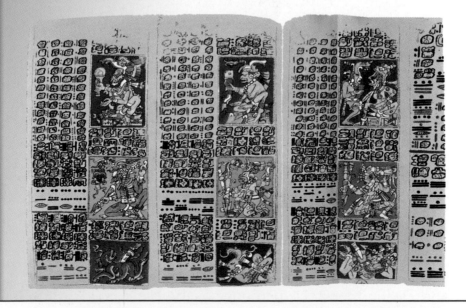

Flint was used to make cutting tools. This is a ceremonial instrument, which depicts a god and two lords in a monster-headed canoe.

material of the Maya, they were found in most lowland areas. But the granite for grinding stones—the metate and the mano—used to produce the zacan, or corn dough that was the staple food of the Maya, was brought to lowland sites from the highlands of present-day Guatemala and the mountains of western Belize.

Similarly, the volcanic glass known as obsidian was an item of trade that was found chiefly in the rocky outcroppings of the Guatemalan highlands. As the sharpest and most durable of cutting materials, it was prized for lances and other weapons of war and was fashioned into knives for household use and for cutting out the hearts of sacrificial victims.

While most lowland sites grew some cotton for basic articles of clothing, the chief source of this fiber and of henequen was the Yucatán Peninsula. Henequen, or sisal, which grew best in the northern lowlands, was vital for the manufacture of ropes and nets used in haulage, building construction, and fishing. Even the tumplines that secured the burdens of the merchants and traders to their backs were woven of this strong, coarse fiber.

Trade After the Collapse of the Classic Period

A severe decline in trade among the city-states of the Classic Period is sometimes offered as one of the reasons for their collapse. Yet the exchange of goods among the Postclassic Maya appears to have taken on new life and a high degree of sophistication, especially in connection with their non-Maya neighbors in Mexico.

Our best evidence of this is the encounter of the party of Christopher Columbus with a large Maya trading canoe that took place in 1502. Columbus was then on his fourth and final journey to the New World. As reported by Columbus's teenage son, the canoe, which was sighted off the coast of present-day Honduras, was carved from a giant tree trunk. It was wide enough to contain a cabin amidships and carried more than two dozen people, including some women and children.

On seizing the canoe and tallying its contents, the Spaniards discovered that the Maya were carrying pottery and colorful cloth garments, flint-studded tools and weapons, wooden swords with obsidian blades, and articles of copper. The canoe also carried a cargo of cacao beans, which the Maya scrambled to save "as if they were their eyes." Although the Spaniards did not seize the Maya trading canoe on this occasion, Maya civilization as it existed in the early 1500s was on its way to extinction.

The Yucatán was the first of the Maya lands to be penetrated by the invading Spaniards. This event took place in 1517, when Francisco Hernández de Córdoba sailed from the island of Cuba to that peninsula of the Mexican mainland in search of slaves. Córdoba died as a result of battle wounds received in this initial bout with the Maya. But reports of gold trinkets found on the Yucatán Peninsula spurred additional expeditions to both the northern and southern lowlands under the command of Hernán Cortés, conqueror of the Aztec Empire of Mexico in 1521.

The life of the Maya was forever changed by their encounters with other peoples in the region, including Spanish explorers.

The infiltration of the Maya regions of habitation, including the southern highlands of Guatemala, was piecemeal throughout the first half of the 1500s. The Spaniards were driven back by pockets of fierce resistance. And disappointment regarding the absence of gold may have weakened their desire for immediate and absolute control. Although the destruction of the final remnants of ancient Maya civilization continued into the following century, the establishment of the Spanish capital city of Mérida on the Yucatán in 1542 may be considered the start of the final phase of the subjugation of the Maya.

Chapter VII

THE LEGACY OF THE ANCIENT MAYA

Today, there are millions of the descendants of the ancient Maya living in Mexico, Guatemala, Honduras, and Belize. The contemporary Maya have been only partially integrated into the western, Christianized culture that resulted from the Spanish conquest. Many still speak remnants of some thirty different Maya languages and retain numerous aspects of the religion, mythology, and folk culture of their forebears.

The legacy of the ancient Maya is also one of widespread significance to the non-Maya world. Primarily, the Maya—especially those of the Classic Period—have bequeathed to us a trove of information about an important segment of the past. Through their art, architecture, and writing, they not only convey the messages of history. They also reveal their achievements in art and technology, ranging from tiny exquisitely incised objects of shell and bone to magnificent, soaring pyramids.

The writing, mathematics, time measurements, and astronomical observations of the Maya tell us that they were capable of sophisticated thought and complicated calculations.

And their belief system reveals a highly imaginative and elaborately constructed view of the world in which they lived. We may not share their beliefs. But at least we are able to know them.

The political, social, and economic aspects of life among the ancient Maya are also part of their legacy. They developed a system of government capable of running powerful city-states for hundreds of years, during which time issues of both trade and warfare had to be carefully balanced if survival was to be ensured.

Some of the ancient Maya rituals are still practiced today by their descendents.

Maya society, however, was sharply divided between the elite and the nonelite, with the former glorifying its personal history in propagandalike detail, while information regarding the lives of the majority of the population went largely unrecorded, to the dismay of social historians.

According to Maya cosmology, there was no distinction between the natural world and the supernatural world. Every aspect of life depended on a set of rigid beliefs and godly dictates, resulting in a political and social system that sanctioned bloodletting, warfare to obtain victims for sacrifices, and human cruelty for the perpetuation of the power of the elite.

Perhaps there is a lesson for contemporary society in the Maya legacy, pointing to the glorious potential of human achievement under thought systems that are unfettered by the dark demands of the unenlightened past.

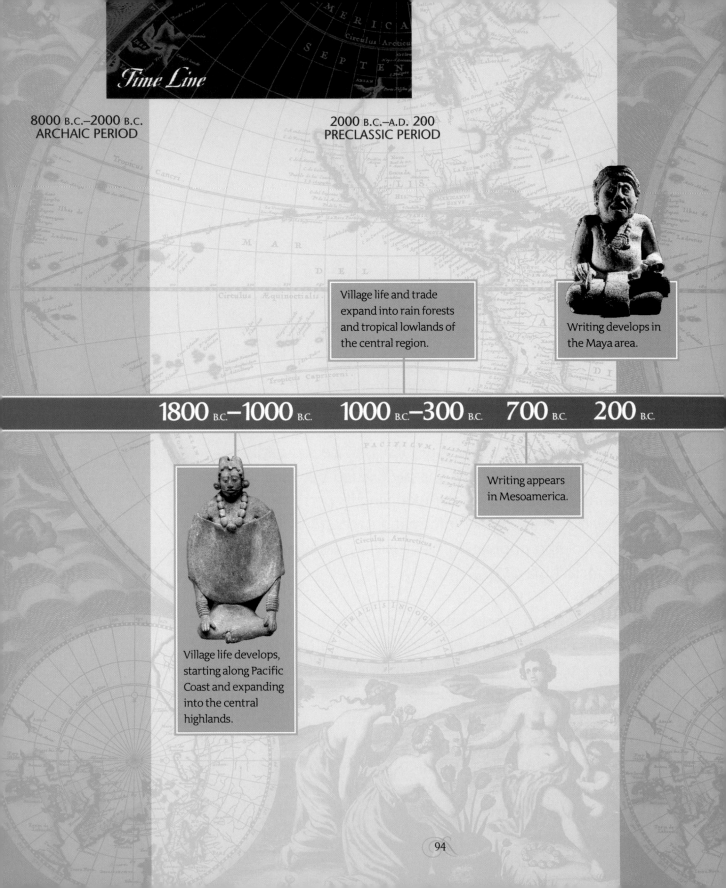

Time Line

8000 B.C.–2000 B.C.
ARCHAIC PERIOD

2000 B.C.–A.D. 200
PRECLASSIC PERIOD

Village life and trade expand into rain forests and tropical lowlands of the central region.

Writing develops in the Maya area.

1800 B.C.–1000 B.C.   **1000 B.C.–300 B.C.**   **700 B.C.**   **200 B.C.**

Writing appears in Mesoamerica.

Village life develops, starting along Pacific Coast and expanding into the central highlands.

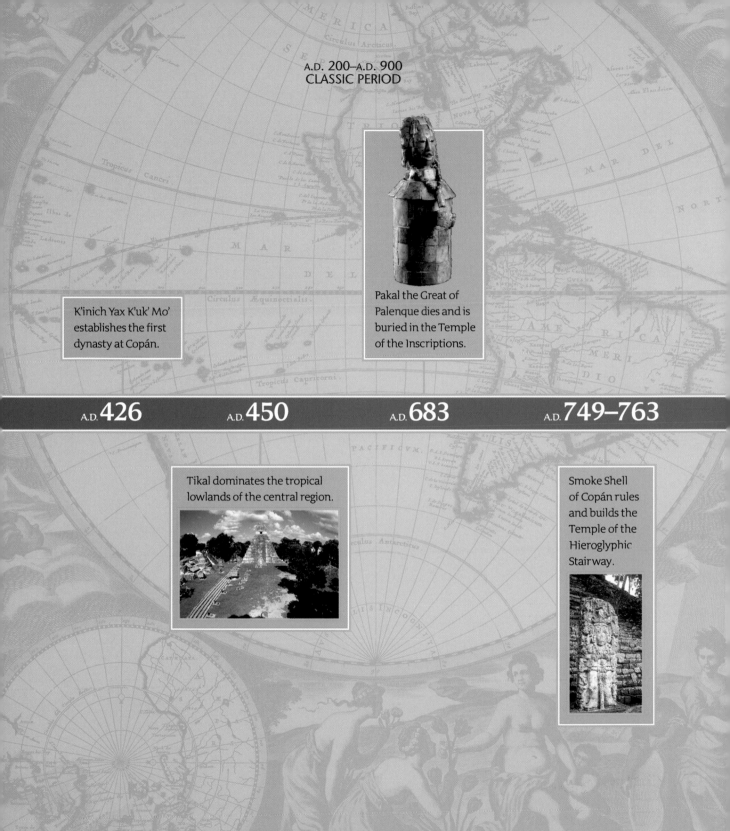

A.D. 200–A.D. 900
CLASSIC PERIOD

K'inich Yax K'uk' Mo' establishes the first dynasty at Copán.

Pakal the Great of Palenque dies and is buried in the Temple of the Inscriptions.

A.D. 426   **A.D. 450**   **A.D. 683**   **A.D. 749–763**

Tikal dominates the tropical lowlands of the central region.

Smoke Shell of Copán rules and builds the Temple of the Hieroglyphic Stairway.

A.D. 200–A.D. 900
CLASSIC PERIOD
(continued)

A.D. 900– A.D. 1500s
POSTCLASSIC PERIOD

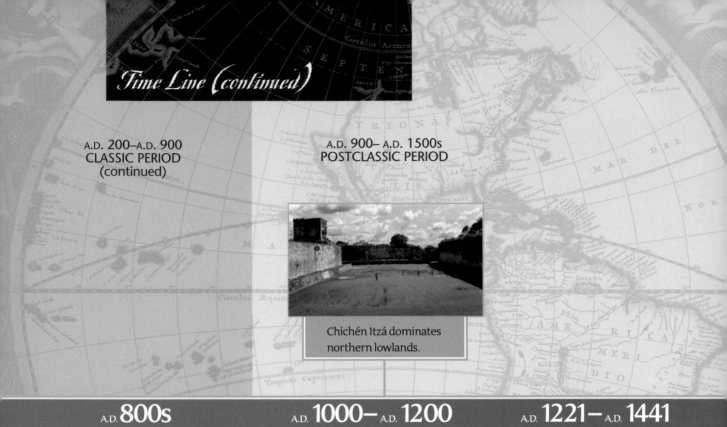

Chichén Itzá dominates
northern lowlands.

A.D. **800s**   A.D. **1000**– A.D. **1200**   A.D. **1221**– A.D. **1441**

Copán, Quiriguá, Tikal,
Calakmul, Palenque,
Yaxchilán, Caracol, and
other sites in the rain
forests and tropical low-
lands, are abandoned.
Northern lowland sites
on the Yucatán Peninsula
continue to flourish
under Toltec influence.

Mayapán holds
sway in the
Yucatán.

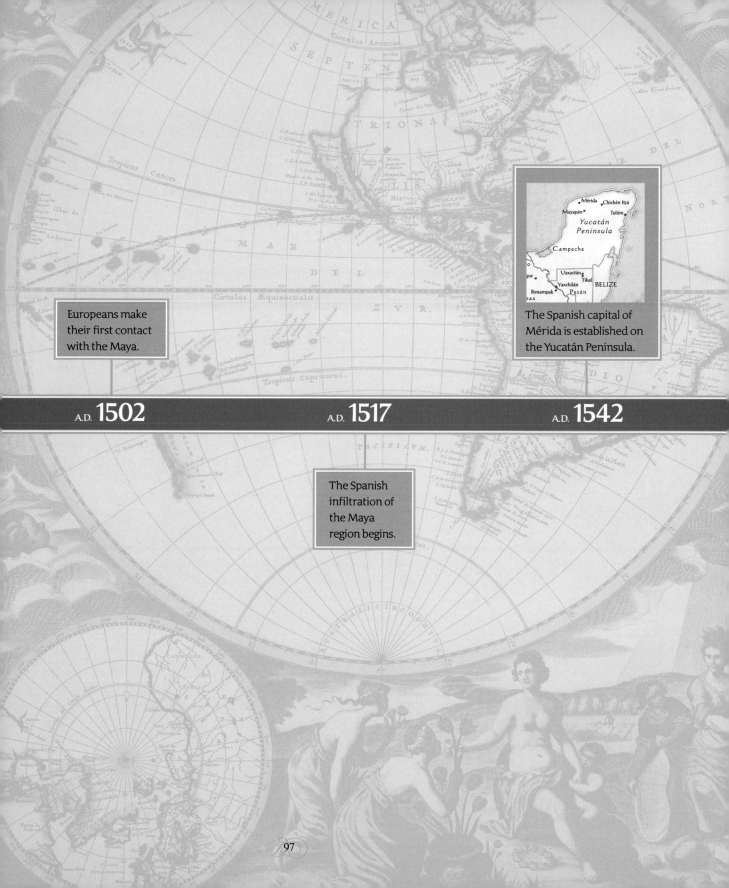

Europeans make
their first contact
with the Maya.

The Spanish capital of
Mérida is established on
the Yucatán Peninsula.

Mérida
Chichén Itzá
Mayapán
Tulúm
Yucatán
Peninsula
Campeche
Uaxactún
Tikal
Yaxchilán
BELIZE
Bonampak
Petén

A.D. **1502**

A.D. **1517**

A.D. **1542**

The Spanish
infiltration of
the Maya
region begins.

Bird Jaguar

Ruled 752–768

Also known as Yaxun B'alam IV, he was the son of Shield Jaguar, most powerful ruler of Yaxchilán, and one of his lesser wives, Lady Ik' Skull of Calakmul. He continued his father's tradition of documenting scenes of royal bloodletting on carved stone lintels. Bird Jaguar was already forty-three years old when he acceded to the throne.

Cauac Sky

Ruled 724–785

Also known as K'ak Tiliw Chan Yopaat, he was the ruler of Quiriguá, a smaller neighbor of Copán that was located a short distance to its north in present-day Guatemala. During his rule, Quiriguá became prosperous, due in part to its favorable position on a river trade route. Cauac Sky attacked Copán and captured and beheaded its ruler, 18 Rabbit.

Chaan Muwaan

Ruled A.D. 700s

He ruled the small site of Bonampak, located in the present-day Mexican state of Chiapas. He is known chiefly for the remarkable painted murals dating from 790 that adorned three rooms of a small structure on the main plaza. The brilliantly colored murals depict the presentation of Chaan Muwaan's son and heir at court, prisoners of war brought before the king, and a royal bloodletting at court.

18 Rabbit

Ruled 695–738

Also known as Waxaklajuun Ub'aah K'awiil, or Ruler 13, of Copán, he reigned for more than forty years before he died at the hands of Cauac Sky, the king of neighboring Quiriguá. The capture and decapitation of 18 Rabbit was considered the worst possible fate that could befall a Maya ruler.

Jaguar Paw 1

Ruled 360–378

Also known as Chak Tok' Ich'aak I, he was king of the prominent city-state of Tikal, located in the jungle lowland region of present-day Guatemala. He was overthrown and killed by ambassadors from Teotihuacán.

Jasaw Chan K'awiil 1

Ruled 682–734

He was the ruler who restored the city-state of Tikal to greatness after the inroads suffered at the hands of its rival, Calakmul, during the A.D. 500s and 600s. He reigned for fifty-two years. His magnificent pyramid tomb in the Temple of the Giant Jaguar was discovered in 1960.

K'an II

Ruled 618–658

He was the ruler of Caracol, an extensive site in the rain forest of present-day western Belize, during its peak years of growth and prosperity. Unlike its neighbors of the Classic Period, Caracol appears to have had a "middle class" that enjoyed such privileges as burial in masonry tombs, which were elsewhere reserved for kings and high-ranking members of the elite.

K'inich Janaab' Pakal

Ruled 615–683

Also known as Pakal the Great, he was ruler of Palenque in the tropical rain forest of the present-day Mexican state of Chiapas. He is best known for his magnificent tomb, rich with jade and other treasures, in the Temple of the Inscriptions, which was painstakingly excavated in 1952.

Lady K'ab'al Xook

She was the principal wife of Shield Jaguar, ruler of Yaxchilán from 681 to 742. Notable examples of stone carvings at the site are the temple lintels that portray Lady K'ab'al Xook performing the sacrifice of bloodletting. In one scene she draws a thorn-studded rope through her tongue. In another she seeks the hallucinatory image of the Vision Serpent by burning bark paper covered with droplets of her blood.

Lady Yohl Ik'nal

Ruled 583–604

Lady Yohl Ik'nal of Palenque was one of the few female rulers of the Maya city-states to have had any real authority during her reign. She became queen due to the absence of a male heir and was the grandmother of Pakal the Great. In 599, Palenque was shaken by an assault at the hands of the king of Calakmul.

Shield Jaguar

Ruled 681–742

Also known as Itzamnaaj B'alam II, he was the powerful warrior king who ruled Yaxchilán, located in the present-day Mexican state of Chiapas. His sixty-year rule was marked by vigorous growth in monument building and trade. The latter was due to Yaxchilán's favorable location on the Usumacinta River. Stone lintels in the temples of Yaxchilán show Shield Jaguar as the successful captor of the lords of neighboring city-states.

Smoke Imix

Ruled 628–695

Also known as K'ak' Unahb' K'awiil or Ruler 12, he was the longest-ruling king of the great Classic Period site of Copán, located in the jungle uplands of present-day Honduras. During his reign great monuments and stelae were erected.

Smoke Shell

Ruled 749–763

As known as K'ak' Yipyaj Chan K'awiil or Ruler 15 of Copán, he attempted to obliterate the memory of the capture and death of 18 Rabbit, or Ruler 13, by building the famed Temple of the Hieroglyphic Stairway. The main purpose of the temple, with its 2,200 stairway glyphs, was to honor the glorious days of Smoke Imix, Ruler 12.

Yuknoom Ch'een II

Ruled 636–686

Also known as Yuknoom the Great, he ruled Calakmul in the rain forest of the present-day Mexican state of Campeche. During the A.D. 600s, Calakmul fought with Tikal for supremacy in the jungle lowlands. Although its structures are badly eroded Calakmul offers evidence of having been an extensive and militarily powerful site.

b'alche   intoxicating fermented corn drink flavored with the bark of the b'alche tree

cenote   a deep well filled with groundwater in the broken limestone surface of the Yucatán Peninsula of Mexico

Chacmool   Toltec-inspired rain god of the Postclassic Maya portrayed as a sinister reclining figure demanding offerings

codex   (plural: codices) ancient manuscript made of bark paper or animal skin

Haab'   the 365-day year of the Maya calendar generally used to mark civic and historic events

hieroglyph   symbol representing an object, an idea, a syllable, or a sound, combined to form a complete writing system

h'men   Maya healer who administered natural medicines as well as spiritual advice based on prophecies

Kukulcán   Postclassic Maya god portrayed as a fanged serpent with the body of a large feathered bird; derived from Quetzalcoatl, a god of non-Maya central Mexico

lintel   horizontal stone or wood support spanning a door or window opening

mano   stone rolling pin for mashing corn kernels into a dough called *zacan*

metate   large, flat stone on which moistened corn kernels are mashed and rolled into a dough with a mano

nacom   executioner at human sacrifices, expert at slashing open the chest of the victim to remove the still-beating heart

obsidian   hard volcanic glass that can be sharpened to a keen cutting edge for knives, spears, and other tools and weapons

quetzal   bird native to the cloud forests of the Guatemalan highlands

stela   (plural: stelae) free-standing stone pillar or slab

Tzolk'in   260-day sacred or religious calendar of the Maya

zacan   dough of corn made by rolling ripe, moistened kernels on a metate with a mano

Books

Day, Nancy. *Your Travel Guide to Ancient Mayan Civilization.* Minneapolis: Runestone/Lerner, 2001.

Galvin, Irene Flum. *The Ancient Maya.* Tarrytown, New York: Marshall Cavendish, 1997.

Meyer, Caroline and Charles Gallenkamp. *The Mystery of the Ancient Maya.* New York: Margaret K. McElderry Books/Simon & Schuster, Revised edition, 1995.

Netzley, Patricia D. *Maya Civilization.* San Diego, California: Lucent Books, 2002.

Odijk, Pamela. *The Mayas.* Englewood Cliffs, New Jersey: Silver Burdett, 1990.

Trout, Lawana Hooper. *The Maya.* New York: Chelsea House, 1991.

Organizations and Online Sites

Maya Adventure
http://www.smm.org/sln/ma/

Produced by the Science Museum of Minnesota, this Web site offers visitors a wealth of information on many Maya sites.

Maya Ruins
http://www.mayaruins.com

This site takes visitors on a photographic tour of several Maya archaeological sites.

Mystery of the Maya
http://www.civilization.ca/civil/maya/mminteng.html

Created by the Canadian Museum of Civilization, students can learn about many aspects of Maya culture and history from this informative site.

Peabody Museum of Archaeology and Ethnology
Harvard University
11 Divinity Street
Cambridge, MA
http://www.peabody.harvard.edu

On its Web site, it is possible to view Altar Q from Copán.

Index

About the Author

Lila Perl is the author of nearly sixty books of both fiction and nonfiction, mainly for readers in the middle grades and for young adults. Her recent nonfiction includes several titles dealing with the social and cultural history of the United States, and a study and analysis of the history of terrorism.

As background for *The Ancient Maya*, Lila Perl has visited the Classic Period site of Palenque in the Mexican state of Chiapas, as well as Chichén Itzá and several other Postclassic sites on the Yucatán Peninsula. She has also investigated Tikal and Quirigua in Guatemala and has written extensively about Maya culture, ancient and modern, in that Central American country. Information about the Maya past is included in her books, *Mexico: Crucible of the Americas* and *Guatemala: Central America's Living Past*, both published by William Morrow and Company.

Lila Perl has received two American Library Association Notable Awards. Nine of her titles have been selected as Notable Children's Trade Books in the Field of Social Studies. Ms. Perl has received a *Boston Globe Horn Book* award, a Sidney Taylor Committee award, and a Young Adults' Choice award from the International Reading Association. The New York Public Library has cited several of her titles among its Best Books for the Teen Age.

Lila Perl holds a Bachelor of Arts degree from Brooklyn College and lives in Beechhurst, New York.